MIKE LIEBERTHAL • CARLOS RUIZ • SMOKY BURGESS •
HOME • EDDIE WAITKUS • CHASE UTLEY
S • MANNY TRILLO • JIMMY ROLLINS • LARRY BOWA
• MIKE SCHMIDT • DICK ALLEN • SCOTT ROLEN • WILLIE
• GREG LUZINSKI • PAT BURRELL • SHERRY MAGEE •
RY MADDOX • TONY GONZALEZ • CHUCK KLEIN • SAM
AVATH • JOHNNY CALLISON • ROBIN ROBERTS • PETE
HILLING • STEVE CARLTON • CHRIS SHORT • CLIFF LEE
EVE BEDROSIAN • TUG MCGRAW • BRAD LIDGE • JOSE
CH • DANNY OZARK • EDDIE SAWYER • BOB BOONE •
• CARLOS RUIZ • SMOKY BURGESS • RYAN HOWARD •
US • CHASE UTLEY • NAPOLEON LAJOIE • JUAN SAMUEL
Y ROLLINS • LARRY BOWA • GRANNY HAMNER • DAVEY
EN • SCOTT ROLEN • WILLIE JONES • PINKY WHITNEY •
BURRELL • SHERRY MAGEE • RICHIE ASHBURN • CY
GONZALEZ • CHUCK KLEIN • SAM THOMPSON • ELMER
ALLISON • ROBIN ROBERTS • PETE ALEXANDER • JIM
ARLTON • CHRIS SHORT • CLIFF LEE • CURT SIMMONS •
TUG MCGRAW • BRAD LIDGE • JOSE MESA • CHARLIE

FEW AND CHOSEN

Defining Phillies Greatness Across the Eras

Gary Matthews

with Phil Pepe

TRIUMPH
B O O K S

Library of Congress Cataloging-in-Publication Data

Matthews, Gary, 1950–
    Few and chosen : defining Phillies greatness across the eras / Gary Matthews
with Phil Pepe.
        p. cm.
    Includes index.
    ISBN 978-1-60078-658-7
    1. Philadelphia Phillies (Baseball team) 2. Baseball players—United States—
Biography. I. Pepe, Phil. II. Title.
    GV875.P45M378 2012
    796.357'640974811—dc23

                                    2011051424

This book is available in quantity at special discounts for your group or organization. For further information, contact:

Triumph Books LLC
542 South Dearborn Street
Suite 750
Chicago, Illinois 60605
(312) 939-3330
Fax (312) 663-3557
www.triumphbooks.com

Printed in U.S.A.
ISBN: 978-1-60078-658-7

Design by Nick Panos; page production by Patricia Frey
All photos courtesy of AP Images unless otherwise noted

Contents

Foreword

My relationship with Gary Matthews goes back many years. I actually knew about him long before he ever knew me. I followed his career when I was director of the minor leagues and scouting for the Phillies under Paul Owens and Sarge was playing for the San Francisco Giants and then the Atlanta Braves. Paul liked players who were so-called "gamers" and Sarge's reputation was just that; he played the game with passion and heart and soul and with his head.

We kept our eye on Sarge and, in 1981, when I was managing the Phillies, we had a chance to get him from the Braves, which I enthusiastically endorsed. We had won the World Series the previous year but figured we needed another big bat in the middle of our lineup to repeat. So we traded Bob Walk, a right-handed pitcher, for Sarge, and that was the first time I met him.

One may remember that 1981 was the year of the baseball strike. It came on June 12, lasted through the month of July, and the season resumed with the All-Star Game in Cleveland on August 9. The powers that be in Major League Baseball had decided that the season would be played in two halves. In each of the four divisions, the teams that finished first in each half-season would meet in a five-game playoff for the right to move on to the league championship series in a best-of-seven playoff.

When the strike hit, we were in first place in the National League East, a game and a half ahead of the Cardinals, so that meant we were assured of playing in the postseason. The Montreal Expos finished first in the second half, the Cardinals again were second, and we were third. By strike-shortened season rules, we were paired with the Expos in the division series. The Cardinals, who finished second in each half-season but had the best overall record in our division, were shut out of the playoffs.

Meanwhile, Sarge had been everything for us that we knew he would be. He played in 101 of our 107 games, batted .301, hit nine home runs, drove in 67 runs, played hard, and was a positive presence in our clubhouse. Through no fault of his, we lost the playoff to the Expos, three games to two. Sarge held up his end, batting .400 in the five games and hitting a huge home run in Game 4. With the Expos ahead two games to one and the score tied 4–4 in the sixth inning, Sarge put us ahead with a home run. We wound up winning the game 6–5 in ten innings to force a sudden-death Game 5, but we lost that game and were eliminated.

I left the Phillies after that season and took over as general manager of the Cubs in 1982. Chicago was a young team trying to rebuild, and we didn't do very well in my first two years. I felt we lacked a veteran presence, so when Sarge was available, knowing firsthand what he brought to the table, knowing his clubhouse presence and how he played the game, I jumped at the chance to get him. My goal in Chicago was to go after guys who knew what winning was all about, who knew what it took to play championship baseball. Sarge was a big part of that. Along with a few other guys, he was the heart and soul of the Cubs team that won the National League East in 1984.

Now Sarge and I have come full circle, both of us back with the Phillies—me as senior adviser, Sarge as a television analyst—and we're able to resume our relationship. I have always enjoyed being around Sarge. He's a true baseball guy. He's been in baseball most of his life—as I have—as a player, a minor league and major league hitting instructor, a broadcaster…and now an author. He's a good man and a great friend.

Sarge and I always seemed to buddy up when we went to spring training. He always was special to me because of the way he played the game and I found that we had similar opinions about players and the way baseball should be played. His passion for the game is second to none. I feel a strong bond with guys who are like that—have a great work ethic and character and pride in what they're doing. I tried to sell that wherever I went. It was easy to sell those ideas to Sarge. As a player, he was the epitome of everything I cherished and everything I was talking about. We got along famously and still do.

I guess to some degree Sarge and I are old school because we think the game should be played a certain way. Obviously in today's game, with the money, free agency, and agents, it gets slightly clouded from time to time. But when you look back at the history of baseball, it's guys like Sarge who still make the game go around and always will.

Sometimes the big-name guys, the superstars, don't want to lower themselves and take a pay cut to stay in the game once their playing days are over. As a result, baseball loses good people who have knowledge of the game and can make an important contribution by giving back. Sarge is not one of those people. He gives back. He's making his contribution. He has added a lot to the Phillies broadcasts with his knowledge of baseball and of the team. He's affable and he's not a status seeker. He won't pass anyone up. Everybody who comes in contact with Sarge loves to hear him talk and loves to talk with him. And he's not one to turn anyone down. He has added a lot to the Phillies broadcasts, so it doesn't surprise me that he has taken on this challenge of selecting his all-time Phillies team.

One thing I know about Sarge is that he will choose players who play the game the way he played it: the right way, with passion. And he won't pick players out of friendship. That's why I'm humbled, honored, and flattered that he has seen fit to include me among such Philadelphia greats as Grover Cleveland Alexander, Robin Roberts, Richie Ashburn, Mike Schmidt, Steve Carlton, and Ryan Howard.

I hope you enjoy reading his book.

—Dallas Green

Preface

Iam proud to say that it was none other than Pete Rose, bless him, who pinned the nickname "Sarge" on me. It happened in 1983.

When I joined the Phillies before the start of the 1981 season (in a trade from the Atlanta Braves for pitcher Bob Walk), Pete was already there. Two years earlier he had signed with the Phillies as a free agent. We were teammates for three seasons.

We finished first in the National League East in 1983 and faced the Dodgers in the National League Championship Series when, after a mediocre regular season (a .258 average, 10 home runs, and 50 RBIs in 132 games), I went on a hot streak. In four games I batted .429, hit three home runs, drove in eight runs, and was named Most Valuable Player of the NLCS.

That's when Pete dubbed me with the nickname "Sarge" and said, "Any time a future Hall of Famer gives you a nickname, it sticks."

Pete got one part right. It's been two decades, and to everybody in baseball (and many outside of it) I'm still known as Sarge, and the name has given me an identity, an image, and a legacy.

But Pete was wrong about the "future Hall of Famer" part. Rose is not in the Hall of Fame, although he should be. I'll deal with that later, but for now, suffice it to say that Pete is one of my favorite teammates. I love Pete Rose. You'll never, ever hear anything negative from me about him.

It's especially flattering to me that my nickname came from a guy who was the ultimate competitor: Pete Rose. Charlie Hustle. Pete honors me because the name implies leadership, competitiveness, determination, a winner. I have always prided myself on being a grinder, someone who gave his all and played hard every day, all day.

I played 16 seasons in the major leagues, was National League Rookie of the Year in 1973, an All-Star in 1979, had 2,011 hits, 234 home runs, and 978 runs batted in. But what I am proudest of is a 10-year span from 1973 to 1982 (including the strike year, 1981) when I played in no fewer than 148 games eight times, and in 1,425 out of a possible 1,561 games, or 91 percent of my team's games.

Besides my nickname, I'm also known in and out of baseball circles for my collection of fedoras. People know me as the guy who likes wearing hats. For as far back as I can remember, I've worn a hat. I'm not sure how many hats I own, probably more than 100; I've lost count. I have boxes of hats everywhere. I have hats for every occasion. I have hats for formal wear, straw hats for the summer, cloth hats for the winter. It's been years since I walked out of my house without a hat on my head.

Because we have learned that the rays of the sun are harmful and can cause skin cancer, many men wear hats today to keep the sun off themselves. But back in the old days, before we learned about the sun's harmful rays, men wore hats to make a fashion statement. A man wasn't dressed properly if he wasn't wearing a hat. That's what I learned growing up.

Times have changed. When you look at films from the '40s and '50s, everybody was wearing a hat, men and women—and not only in the stands. The players wore hats when they went out to the various clubs around town after the game. Mostly, hats were worn as a fashion statement and boy, did they look good. I look forward every year to the Kentucky Derby to see the fashion parade of hats. There are some that go overboard, but there are some, especially the ones worn by the women, that make you turn your head.

In recent years I began designing my own hats. As a matter of fact, I may have the opportunity, and the honor, of designing a hat for President Obama. Let me explain.

In 2003 Dusty Baker became manager of the Chicago Cubs and asked me to be his hitting instructor. Naturally, I accepted. I had never played on the same team with Dusty; we had known each other only as opponents over the years. I was flattered that he would choose me as his hitting instructor.

At the time, Barack Obama was a civil rights attorney in Chicago who also taught constitutional law at the University of Chicago Law School. Coincidentally, President Obama's daughter Malia attended the same dance class as my daughter Paige. The girls' mothers knew each other previously, but as the girls got a little older, they played on soccer teams together and their friendship grew. The two girls became friends, and that brought their mothers together, too. One thing led to another and that's how I met the president-to-be.

The Cubs trained in Arizona, and the future president and future first lady, Michelle, would come there during spring training. Dusty would occasionally have cookouts at his house, and he usually would invite me. Once he invited me when the Obamas were in town, and I mentioned to Dusty that I'd like to bring them along to the cookout.

That's how I got better acquainted with the president. Don't get me wrong, I'm not saying we're best friends or anything. For instance, I never was one of his basketball-playing buddies, but I did get to play golf with him.

Obama was president when the 2008 Phillies won the World Series and the team was invited to the White House for a reception in 2009. As a member of the broadcast team, I was invited along with them. The president greeted the players in the Rose Garden, shook hands with them, and made a little small talk. I was standing in the front during his speech, and he spotted me there. When he finished his talk, the president looked at me and said, "Hey, what's up, Sarge? How are you doing?" And he came over and gave me a hug.

After Obama was elected president, I did some research and learned that there were two U.S. presidents who were known for wearing hats: Abraham Lincoln, of course, wore his familiar stovepipe hat. And Franklin D. Roosevelt wore that fedora on which he turned down both the front and back brims. That gave me an idea.

In 2010 I was privileged to be included among a small group of 35 or so friends and acquaintances of the president invited to Thanksgiving dinner at the White House. I took advantage of the opportunity to mention to Obama that the last U.S. president to wear a hat was FDR. I said, "Mr. President, why don't you wear a hat once in a while? I'll even design one for you." And he said, "If I make it in next time, I'll consider doing it."

My plan is to design a couple of hats for him, maybe a brown one and a black one, and I'll let the

Visiting President
Obama in 2010.

first lady know and hopefully, she'll take it from there. If the president starts wearing a hat, that will jump start the hat industry like you can't believe. Maybe I'll even get a cabinet post out of it. I can picture it: Gary Matthews, secretary of hats! Or maybe Gary Matthews, sergeant in charge of hats!

Only in America can a kid born and raised in San Fernando, California, into a family not too far above the poverty line, not only become a Major League Baseball player but also get to meet the president of the United States.

I'm the oldest of three boys, the three of us separated by only three years, so you can imagine what that must have been like for my mother. My mom and dad met and married in Alabama. They worked hard—my dad in construction, my mom cleaning houses—and when they had saved enough money, they left Alabama and headed for California, settling in the San Fernando Valley area, where my dad had relatives. Poultry farms were plentiful in and around San Fernando, so there was work available. So that's where my folks settled and purchased a small, modest house.

The only house I knew before I left home to play baseball was a one-family dwelling with two bedrooms; my two brothers and I shared one of them. The house was small, but it was comfortable, and we even had our own backyard. The neighborhood we lived in was mixed—blacks, whites, Hispanics, Asians, Jews, Irish, Italians. A real melting pot!

Because of my upbringing I never knew any prejudice as a kid. And by the time I started in pro baseball, most of the barriers had fallen. For the most part, black and white players lived in the same hotels and ate in the same restaurants. The first time I experienced any prejudice was in Little Rock, Arkansas, as a visiting player in my third year as a professional. I was called a lot of names I hadn't heard before. Because of my background, it was all new to me and a shock to my system.

For the first time I had some understanding of what Jackie Robinson must have gone through as the first African American to play in the major leagues, living apart from the rest of the Brooklyn Dodgers, either in a hotel in the Negro section of town or with African American families, not allowed to take meals where his teammates ate. Fortunately, I never had to experience any of that firsthand.

My experience in Little Rock was only a small part of what Robinson went through. Nevertheless it gave me an idea of what he had endured and it made me appreciate the sacrifices he made for the betterment of those who came after him. I don't know if I would have had the strength and the courage to endure what he did. There's no question that in Jackie Robinson, baseball had the right man to break the color barrier.

When I was three years old, my mom and dad decided to take the family on vacation to Alabama to visit relatives. We all piled into the family car and began the long journey, my dad driving on retreaded tires. One of the tires blew, and we were in a serious accident. My dad was killed instantly. My two brothers were unhurt, but I had a broken leg. My mom's neck was broken. When she recovered, she was left alone to raise three boys, all of us three years old or younger.

My mom, Catherine, who passed on a few years ago, was my all-time hero, a person of rare courage and strength. She was both mother and father to us as well as our inspiration, counselor, teacher, minister, and disciplinarian. Mom worked at a variety of jobs—janitorial work at the local schools, cooking, cleaning, washing clothes. She took whatever odd jobs she could get to support us.

We were by no means rich, but we never wanted for anything. We ate a lot of oatmeal and chicken, but there were no sad stories for me. My childhood, except for not having a dad, was a normal and happy one. Not knowing our dad, we just thought that was the natural order of things. It was always Mom. She was always there, supporting us and providing for us. She sacrificed and never took another vacation the rest of her life.

One reason my mom never took a vacation is because of my involvement in sports. I was always playing one sport or another year-round. My mom always supported me and encouraged me. She came to as many of my games as she could when she wasn't working. She didn't know a lot about sports, but she told me she could always tell from several blocks away whether my team won or lost by the way I was walking.

When my brothers and I were old enough we were expected to do what we could to pitch in and help earn extra money by taking on odd jobs. I had a paper route for a while. I also sold *Jet* magazine. I could go to the local barbershop on a Saturday and get rid of my entire supply of magazines.

I always worked at one job or another, helping out with the family finances, but I still managed to find time to compete in sports. When I was in high school, I had a job at the Veterans Hospital developing X-rays. They would send the X-rays in to me. The room I was in had to be dark during the development process, so to keep myself occupied and avoid going stir crazy, I brought my tape recorder and my tapes. Mostly, I had tapes of my favorite singer, Stevie Wonder, and I listened to them over and over until I memorized the lyrics of all his songs and I still remember those lyrics to this day.

"My Cherie Amour...."

In high school, I was picked to do a television commercial for Hunt's tomato sauce. My coach was asked to choose two players for an audition, and I was one of them. I went to the audition, and the producers had me walk in front of the camera and speak a few lines and I was picked for the commercial. It ran for a while in our area. I not only got paid for shooting the commercial, I also received residuals.

One incident when I was young that I'll never forget involves my mom exacting her own special brand of justice and discipline. Mom sang in the church choir, and we were expected to go with her to church every Sunday and sit quietly waiting for her until the service was over. Being restless and having a short attention span—typical of most kids—one day I pinched my brother and he screamed out, his screams reverberating throughout the church.

The pastor was in the middle of his sermon at the time and he stopped and said, "You Matthews boys, come on down and sit in these front-row seats." So the three of us got up and moved down front. As we did, we looked at the choir and there was my mother staring at us with a look that was unmistakable. The three of us just lowered our heads because we knew we were in for trouble.

When we got home, Mom gave us a choice: we could either spend the remainder of the day in the house or we could go outside and pick our own switch off the tree so we could get what was coming to us—and it had better be a switch that didn't break, no skinny switches allowed. I chose the switch because I wanted to go out and play.

As a kid, and later in high school, I played three sports: baseball, football, and basketball. Buddy Bradford, an outfielder who played 11 seasons with the White Sox, Indians, Cardinals, and Reds, was my next-door neighbor and something of a role model and hero for me. He was a few years ahead of me at San Fernando High School, which also produced football players Anthony Davis and Charles White, both of whom were a few years younger than me. In high school I played in the same division as Doug DeCinces, who went to Monroe High, one of our rivals, and later was a star third baseman for the Baltimore Orioles and California Angels. We would beat them in basketball and they would beat us in baseball.

In football, I was a wide receiver on offense and a linebacker on defense, but my burgeoning football career came to a sudden end one July day. I got discouraged because we were doing two-a-day workouts, and the Valley in July is not a good place to be with that helmet on your head. So I took my pads off and never went back to football.

I was a decent basketball player. I made All-State and played against Curtis Rowe and Sidney Wicks, both of whom went on to win three national championships under John Wooden at UCLA. I probably could have played basketball in college somewhere, but I remembered going up for a shot against Sidney Wicks and he slapped the ball off my head. I decided right there that basketball was not a good sport for me.

Baseball was my game, even though I wasn't one of those players who batted over .500, hit many long home runs, and was all-world in high school. I was a good player, all-conference, and I was consistent. The big thing is that I played a lot of baseball. Because of the Southern California weather I was able to play baseball practically year-round. I'd play on my high school team, and in the summer I'd play American Legion ball. I was playing close to 100 games per year, which was a big thing in my development and improvement. In high school I played third base, hit third in the lineup, and always hit better than .300. By the time I reached my senior year I had grown to practically my full 6'2" height and 190 pounds. I batted about .333 as a senior and was beginning to get noticed by major-league scouts.

George Genovese was the scout for the Giants in our area. He signed George Foster, Jack Clark, Jim Barr, Dave Kingman, and Garry Maddox—and he took a chance on me. The Giants made me their first-round pick, 17th overall, right out of high school in the 1968 amateur draft. I signed for a bonus of $35,000.

The first thing I did was what every bonus baby in the '60s did: I bought a car, a '69 Buick Riviera. I went shopping in Culver City, walked into the showroom, and said, "That's the one I want, right there." It took me five minutes. I wrote a check on the spot, I think it was $3,000, maybe $3,500, and *see you later*. I drove the car out of the showroom. What a car! I loved that car. I drove it all through my years in the minor leagues, drove it to spring training and to Decatur, Illinois, to start my pro career with the Decatur Commodores in the Class A Midwest League in 1969.

At Decatur, my manager was Frank Funk. One of my teammates was Leo Mazzone, who would later earn a reputation as a pitching guru when he was pitching coach for the Atlanta Braves, where he tutored that great staff which included Greg Maddux, Tom Glavine, and John Smoltz. The Giants had moved me to the outfield. That first year, I tore cartilage in my knee and played in only 53 games with Decatur, in which I batted .322 with eight home runs. Dr. Frank Jobe did the operation on my knee. The Vietnam War was on at the time, and I received my draft notice. I showed up on crutches and was given a medical exemption, so the injury actually kept me from possibly going off to fight overseas.

The next year I was moved up to Fresno in the California League, where I batted .279 with 23 homers and 74 RBIs. After Fresno there was a year at Double A Amarillo and a year at Triple A Phoenix until I reached San Francisco and made my major-league debut on September 6, 1972.

I consider myself blessed to have played in the big leagues for 16 seasons and 2,033 games, all but 45 of those games in the National League with four of the most storied franchises in baseball history: the Giants, Braves, Phillies, and Cubs.

I enjoyed my time with all four teams, but being traded to the Phillies was special because it gave me the opportunity to play in my only World Series, in 1983. That's why I was excited when the Phillies brought me back in 2007 to be part of their broadcast team and why I was eager to take on the challenge of selecting my all-time Phillies team.

These are my choices, and the team is my team, unofficial and not one selected by the Phillies or their fans. My goal was to choose players based not on their entire careers but solely on their performance while playing for Philadelphia.

Making this challenge even more difficult is that, in their almost 130-year history, there have been many great players among the almost 2,000 who have worn the Phillies uniform (35 who wore the uniform have been inducted into the National Baseball Hall of Fame). Obviously I have not seen them all, but I have tried to do my due diligence by examining the records of those who I did not see.

I will, however, admit to a certain bias when it comes to those I have seen, played with, and played against, and I have given them the benefit of any doubt.

—Gary Matthews

Acknowledgments

This book is dedicated to my best friend—my mom, Catherine—and to my daughter, Paige.

Mom was a young woman when she was widowed and left with three little boys when my dad, who I never really knew, was killed in an automobile accident while driving from San Fernando, California, to Alabama, on our way to our first—and last—family vacation. Years later, I learned that despite suffering a broken neck, Mom found the strength and courage to get us three young boys back to our home in San Fernando.

One of the things my mom taught me at an early age was to treat people with respect, and to believe you can do anything in life you want to do. She also taught me not judge people by what others have said about them. She explained that there would be times I'd feel I'm all by myself on an island and, boy, have I ever come to understand that.

I have tried to live my life by the principles instilled in me by my mom, not listening to others, but judging each situation on its own merit. I may not have always succeeded, and that philosophy has gotten me in trouble from time to time. Nevertheless I have no regrets. I've never been a follower, always a leader.

I hope and pray that my daughter Paige will live her life by that same philosophy and that she will follow the principles of my mom, her grandmother, and realize that with hard work she can do anything she wants to do and be whoever she wants to be.

Mom also taught me to respect all women. She preached that disrespecting any woman is like disrespecting your own mother. That principle of mom's permeated my life from the minor leagues to the major leagues and beyond, and I have tried to pass her philosophy on to my own sons. I fervently hope I have been successful in demonstrating my respect for all women to my sons and to any young man I have come in contact with.

I think of my mom most days and especially on Mother's Day. Shortly after mom passed on I was driving to the ballpark on Mother's Day and on the radio came the song, "I'll Always Love My Momma/She's My Favorite Girl." The tears began streaming uncontrollably down my face I had to pull over to the shoulder of the road because I couldn't see the cars in front of me.

After my dad died, Mom dedicated her life to raising her three boys. She never remarried, and any man she let into her life had to accept her three sons.

The sacrifices Mom made for me and my brothers is something I'll never forget. Uneducated and in debt, she was left with three small boys, but with a huge heart and the willingness to work to support her family. That's another reason I'll always love my momma; she's my favorite girl.

This is a book rating the uniformed personnel of the Phillies throughout their history—the players and managers—without mention of others who deserve recognition. There are the owners and general managers who, in some cases, have had as much to do with winning as those who wore the uniform, and the broadcasters, who are as popular in Philadelphia as most players.

I will not list these individuals in any order of preference so as to avoid bruising any egos or hurting any feelings. Instead, I will simply acknowledge them and convey my respect and appreciation for their enormous contribution to Phillies baseball and the city of Philadelphia.

I start by recognizing from the ownership/management level such longtime Phillies executives as the Carpenters—Bob Sr., his son Bob Jr., and his son Ruly—descendants of the wealthy and powerful du Ponts of the Wilmington, Delaware, chemical company. The Carpenters had much to do with laying the groundwork for what today is regarded as among the finest organizations in Major League Baseball.

The Phillies' fortunes rose under general manager Paul Owens, "the Pope," who also took a turn as field manager in 1983 and 1984, and his successor as GM, Bill Giles. The Phillies were ushered into their greatest period of success in 1992 when David Montgomery was named chief operating officer (today he is general partner and president as well as CEO) and reached their pinnacle in 2006 with the arrival of Hall of Fame general manager Pat Gillick and his assistant, later his successor, the Phillies' current GM, Ruben Amaro Jr.

In their history, the Phillies have had almost as glittering an array of radio (and later television) broadcasters as they have Hall of Fame players, including those who were before my time—Byrum Saam, Gene Kelly, and Andy Musser—and those who came later—the legendary Harry Kalas, the incomparable Richie Ashburn, and my contemporaries and colleagues in the booth, Chris Wheeler, Larry Andersen, Scott Franzke, and Tom McCarthy.

Introduction

In light of their recent dominance, it's difficult to fathom that the Philadelphia Phillies are saddled with the ignominious reputation of baseball's most chronic losers—a reputation, unfortunately, that is richly deserved.

Through the 2011 season, the Phillies had earned that distinction by:

- Losing 10,292 games, more than any other team.
- Posting a .473 winning percentage, the fourth-lowest in baseball history. (To add insult to injury, the three lower winning percentages are by expansion teams.)
- Losing 100 or more games in a single season 14 times, more than any other team.
- Finishing last in their league or division 31 times, more than any other team.
- Suffering through 16 consecutive losing seasons (1933–48), a major-league record at the time that has since been surpassed by the Pittsburgh Pirates.
- Losing a major-league-record 23 consecutive games in 1961.
- Experiencing arguably the worst collapse in baseball history in 1964.

Nevertheless, even W.C. Fields would rather be in Philadelphia. And for a whole new generation of avid Phillies fans, redemption is sweet.

The National League's Philadelphia franchise came into existence in 1883 when league president A.G. Mills announced the National League's plan to abandon Troy, New York, and Worcester, Massachusetts, and move those teams to larger cities, targeting New York City and Philadelphia. Upon learning of the impending relocation, sporting goods manufacturer Al Reach and his partner Ben Shibe purchased 50 percent of the Worcester team, joined forces with Pennsylvania attorney John Rogers, who had purchased the other 50 percent, and brought the team to Philadelphia.

In official documents, Philadelphia's new team was called the Phillies, but the city's newspapers insisted on calling them "the Quakers," and Quakers they would remain in print through 1889.

The first game of the Quakers/Phillies franchise was played on May 1, 1883, in Philadelphia's Recreation Park against the powerful Providence Grays. The home team lost 4–3 to the Grays and their star, future Hall of Fame pitcher Charles "Old Hoss" Radbourne, who would win 48 games that season and 59 in 1884.

After that auspicious debut it was all downhill for the Quakers, who finished the season with a record of 17–81 and established an unfortunate trend by coming in last in the eight-team National League, 46 games behind the Boston Beaneaters.

The losing continued into the next millennium for the Phillies. When they had hitting, they didn't have pitching (in 1897 Ed Delahanty batted .377 and drove in 96 runs and Napoleon Lajoie batted .361 and drove in 127, but the top three starting pitchers all had losing records and the Phillies finished in 10th place). And when they had pitching, they didn't have hitting (in 1914 Grover Cleveland "Pete" Alexander won 27 games and Erskine Mayer won 21, but the Phillies had only two batters over .300, three with home runs in double figures, and two with more than 66 RBIs and finished in sixth place with a losing record).

Although they were a first-division team for 11 straight years, from 1885–1895, the Phillies would not finish first until 1915, the 33rd year of their existence. Led by Alexander's 31 wins, the Philadelphians finished seven games ahead of the Boston Braves (née Beaneaters) under rookie manager Pat Moran, but lost the World Series in five games to the Boston Red Sox. (The Phillies would have to wait 35 years before winning another pennant and 65 years before winning their first World Series.)

Two years after reigning as National League champions, the Phillies entered a period that became the bleakest in their history—or the history of any major league team for that matter. In a 31-year span from 1918 to 1948 they would finish in the first division in the eight-team National League just once (fourth place in 1932). They would have 30 losing seasons and finish fifth twice, sixth four times, seventh eight times, and eighth 16 times.

In those 31 seasons, the Phillies would lose 100 games or more 12 times, compile a record of 1,752–2,941 for a winning percentage of .373 (or a losing percentage of .627), and finish an aggregate 1,191½ games out of first place (or an average of 38½ games out per year).

Despite such historic ineptitude, the Phillies of that period did have their moments, and their individual stars, such as Gavvy Cravath, Cy Williams, Eppa Rixey, Chuck Klein, Dolph Camilli, Danny Litwhiler, Curt Davis, and Del Ennis.

Their lack of success on the field did not deter the Phillies from introducing innovations to the game, however. The Phillies and New York Giants were baseball's first teams to use different uniforms for home and away games, and the Phillies, under manager Harry Wright, were the first team to employ pregame batting practice and the first to hit fungos to outfielders in preparation for a game.

Fortified by center fielder Richie Ashburn and pitcher Robin Roberts, a pair of second-year players, the Phillies ended their 31-year drought with a winning record (81–73) and third-place finish in 1949. A year later they ascended to the top of the National League with a team called "the Whiz Kids" because it was made up of so many young players, including 25-year-old outfielder Del Ennis and pitcher Bubba Church; 24-year-old pitcher Bob Miller, catcher Stan Lopata, and third baseman Willie "Puddin' Head" Jones; 23-year-old shortstop Granny Hamner, center fielder Ashburn, and pitcher Roberts; and 21-year-old pitcher Curt Simmons.

The Philly Whiz Kids won the 1950 National League pennant on a three-run home run by Dick Sisler in the tenth inning on the final day of the season in Brooklyn's Ebbets Field, but their hopes for their first World Series championship were dashed when they ran into the powerhouse New York Yankees. The Whiz Kids were no match for the veteran Yankees of Joe DiMaggio, Phil Rizzuto, Yogi Berra, Hank Bauer, Vic Raschi, Allie Reynolds, and Eddie Lopat and were swept in four games, albeit by scores of 1–0, 2–1, 3–2, and 5–2.

A year later, the Phillies slipped to fifth place. They would go 25 years between championships, during which time they would have only nine winning seasons and finish in last place seven times. They also would have to endure for years the lasting ignominy of being the last National League team and the third-to-last major-league team (only the Detroit Tigers and Boston Red Sox came after them) to break baseball's shameful color line. In 1957, 12 years after Jackie Robinson joined the Brooklyn Dodgers, John Kennedy, a 30-year-old infielder from Jacksonville, Florida, became the first African American to wear a home-team major-league uniform in the "City of Brotherly Love." He appeared in five games for the Phillies, batted twice without a hit, struck out once, and was never heard from again.

The decade of the '60s brought more losing and much heartbreak to Philadelphia—two eighth-place finishes, two sevenths, and one sixth. In 1961 the Phillies lost a record 23 consecutive games on their way to finishing with a record of 47–107, 46 games behind Cincinnati.

In 1964 the Phillies held a 6½ game lead with 12 games to play when they proceeded to lose their next 10 games and ended up tied for second place behind the St. Louis Cardinals.

The 1970s brought the Phillies their most successful period in the team's almost 100-year history up to that time, made possible by an influx of fresh, new talent. Larry Bowa and Greg Luzinski arrived in 1970; Mike Schmidt, Bob Boone, and Steve Carlton came aboard in 1972; Jim Lonborg and Dick Ruthven in 1973; Gene Garber in 1974; and Garry Maddox in 1975.

From 1976 to 1983, the Phillies won five division titles, two National League pennants, and the franchise's second World Series—which they took in six games over the Kansas City Royals in 1980.

The greatest period in the history of Phillies baseball, however, has come in the new millennium. From 2001 through 2011, the Phils have finished third twice, second four times, and first for five consecutive years, 2007–11. They have won two pennants and one World Series. This rise has coincided with the arrival of Pat Burrell and Jimmy Rollins in 2000; Placido Polanco and Brett Myers in 2002; Chase Utley and Jim Thome in 2003; Ryan Howard and Billy Wagner in 2004; manager Charlie Manuel and Shane Victorino in 2005; Carlos Ruiz, Cole Hamels, and Jamie Moyer in 2006; Jayson Werth in 2007; Pedro Feliz, Brad Lidge, and Joe Blanton in 2008; Raul Ibanez and Cliff Lee in 2009; and Roy Halladay and Roy Oswalt in 2010.

The Phillies are an elite team with a checkered past. While 34 who wore the Phillies uniform are enshrined in the baseball Hall of Fame in Cooperstown, New York, only a handful (Grover Cleveland Alexander, Richie Ashburn, Steve Carlton, Ed Delahanty, Chuck Klein, Robin Roberts,

Mike Schmidt, and Sam Thompson) earned their plaques primarily because of their accomplishments as Phillies. Others came to the Phillies too soon (Ferguson Jenkins, Casey Stengel, Eppa Rixey, Ryne Sandberg) or too late (Jimmie Foxx, Hack Wilson, Tony Perez, Joe Morgan).

The Phillies have long been a soft landing place for players winding down their careers or those who had excelled elsewhere, such as Gary Matthews. He came to Philadelphia in 1981 in a trade with the Atlanta Braves after five distinguished career in San Francisco, where he was the 1973 National League Rookie of the Year, and four more outstanding years with the Braves.

In three seasons with the Phillies, Matthews batted .301, .281, and .258, hit 38 home runs, and drove in 200 runs; helped the Phillies win one division title and one National League pennant; and was voted Most Valuable Player of the 1983 National League Championship Series when he batted .429, hit three home runs, and drove in eight runs in the four-game victory over the Los Angeles Dodgers. In 16 major-league seasons with the Giants, Braves, Phillies, Cubs, and Mariners, Matthews compiled a creditable lifetime average of .281 with 234 home runs and 978 RBIs.

Matthews is uniquely qualified for the task of selecting the all-time Phillies team. He played 15 of his 16 major-league seasons in the National League and has been a television analyst with the Phillies since 2007. Consequently, many of those who make up his all-time Phillies team are those Matthews played with or against or who he has viewed from his broadcast perch in the press box.

—Phil Pepe

ONE

Catcher

Although I was his teammate for only a few months (I was traded to the Phillies on March 25, 1981, and he was sold by the Phillies to the California Angels eight months and 12 days later), Bob Boone and I have several things in common:

- We both were born and raised in southern California, me in San Fernando, Boone in San Diego, some 125 miles away.
- I was drafted in the first round of the 1968 amateur draft; Boone was drafted a year later.
- I made my major-league debut on September 6, 1972; Bob made his major-league debut four days later.
- We both have had the great joy and enormous pride of seeing our sons follow in our footsteps to play in the major leagues: Bret and Aaron for Boone, Gary Jr. for me. (Not only were Boone's two sons major-leaguers, his father, Ray, also played in the big leagues with the Tigers, Indians, White Sox,

1. BOB BOONE

2. ANDY SEMINICK

3. DARREN DAULTON

4. MIKE LIEBERTHAL

5.-*t* CARLOS RUIZ

5.-*t* SMOKY BURGESS

Bob Boone readies for a game in the 1977 postseason.

Athletics, Braves, and Red Sox, making the Boones one of the few families with three generations in Major League Baseball.)

When Boone retired after the 1990 season, he had caught more games
(2,225, with 1,125 of them as a Phillie) than any other catcher in major-
league history (he would be caught and passed by Carlton Fisk three years
later and by Pudge Rodriguez 16 years after that). He made the All-Star team
four times, won seven Gold Gloves (Rodriguez (13) and Johnny Bench (10),
Boone's contemporary, are the only catchers who won more), and was the
only catcher behind the plate for both a perfect game (pitched by Mike Witt)
and a pitcher's 300th win (Don Sutton).

On August 19, 1992, in Baltimore, Bret Boone made his major-league debut, starting at second base for the Seattle Mariners against the Orioles. In doing so, he became the first third-generation Major League Baseball player, following his grandfather, Ray—a third baseman, shortstop, and first baseman with the Indians, Tigers, Braves, White Sox, Red Sox, and A's (1948–60)—and his father, Bob, who played for the Phillies, Angels, and Royals during his 19-year major-league career. (Another Boone, Bob's son Aaron, arrived in the major leagues with the Reds five years later.)

Subsequently, through 2011, there have been more third-generation major-league families, including one with an asterisk:

- The Bells: Gus, an outfielder with the Pirates, Reds, Expos and Mets in the 1950s and 1960s; his son, Buddy; and Buddy's sons David and Mike.
- The Colemans: Pitchers Joe, Joe Jr., and Casey, respectively.
- The Hairstons: Sammy, son Jerry, and his sons Jerry Jr. and Scott.
- The asterisk and trivia question pertains to the fifth third-generation family, the Schofield/Werths. Ducky Schofield, his son Dick, and Jayson Werth, are all major-leaguers. Werth is the grandson of Ducky Schofield, the nephew of Dick Schofield. and the stepson of Dennis Werth, who was a catcher with the Yankees and Royals from 1979 to 1982.

Not to be outdone, there also is one—and only one—three-generation family of major-league umpires, the Runges: Ed, his son Paul, and Paul's son Brian.

While he wasn't known for his bat—he carries a lifetime average of .254, 105 home runs, and 826 RBIs—whatever he contributed on offense was considered a bonus. Boone, who is the only catcher in the Phillies Wall of Fame, was a fierce competitor who was known more for his defense and his durability than for his offense. He was a student of the game. He was one of those guys who pitchers loved to throw to, although it's interesting to note that

Steve Carlton elected to have Tim McCarver as his personal catcher. I don't know if that was a critique of Boone's ability by Carlton or if it simply was that Steve was comfortable throwing to McCarver, who was his catcher when Lefty broke in with the Cardinals.

[Seminick] was my kind of guy— hard-nosed, a winner, a dogged competitor.

Don Sutton called Boone "one of the most intelligent catchers I've ever seen."

That was Bob's reputation, and deservedly so.

The fact is, in 1980 Boone handled the Phillies pitching staff that won the World Series. Up to that time, no Phillies catcher had ever done that…and it would be 28 more years before another Phillies catcher would do it again.

I truly regret that I never got to know **Andy Seminick**, but even though we never met, I feel like I do know him. I've had two tours of duty with the Phillies—as a player from 1981 to 1983, and as a television broadcaster since 2007—and you can't spend any time around the Phillies without hearing about Seminick or knowing someone who was tutored, coached, scouted, or managed by him.

From what I have heard about him, I would have liked being managed by or playing alongside him. He was my kind of guy—hard-nosed, a winner, a dogged competitor—the kind of guy you would run through a wall for if he was your manager or the one you would want in your foxhole if he was on your team.

Known more for his home-run bat than for his defense, Andy Seminick nevertheless was the Phillies' primary catcher in 1950, guiding a young pitching staff that led the National League in earned-run average (3.50) and was second in shutouts (13). He was instrumental in delivering the franchise's first pennant in 35 years.

Along the way, Seminick caught 124 games, threw out 23 of 58 runners attempting to steal—an exceptional 40 percent (33 percent is considered above average)—batted .288, finished 13th in the National League with 24 homers, drove in 68 runs, and was 14th in the MVP voting.

Perhaps unfairly, what many longtime Phillies fans remember most about Seminick was not his glove, but his bat: 123 home runs and 411 RBIs in 985 games as a Phillie; 48 homers and 136 RBIs over a two-year span, 1949–50; and especially one unforgettable day, June 2, 1949, when the Phillies tied a

Andy Seminick was a leader on the Phillies teams of the 1950s.

major-league record by hitting five home runs in the eighth inning against the Cincinnati Reds. Two of those homers were made by Seminick, who had hit one earlier in the game in the second inning. As we like to say in the dugout, Andy Seminick had a good month that day.

Because he was a 29-year-old, eight-year major-league veteran in 1950, Seminick earned the trust of manager Eddie Sawyer with handling a young pitching staff that included 23-year-old Robin Roberts, 21-year-old Curt Simmons, 24-year-old Bob Miller, 25-year-old Bubba Church, and 26-year-old Russ Meyer. That was the staff for the famous Phillies Whiz Kids.

Consequently, the Philadelphia writers dubbed Seminick "Grandpa Whiz."

Years later Roberts, the great Hall of Famer, said of Seminick, "If you had to pick a guy in our clubhouse who was our leader that year, it would be Andy. He always played hard, and that was his best year."

Sounds like my kind of player.

Although he was born in West Virginia and signed his first professional contract with the Pirates, Seminick was as much a Phillie as any player in the team's history. He was signed as an amateur free agent before the 1940 season, released and signed as a free agent a year later, and then returned to his minor-league club and was purchased by the Phillies from Knoxville of the Southern Association in September 1943.

After the 1951 season Seminick was included in a four-for-three trade with Cincinnati in which the two teams swapped catchers Seminick and Smoky Burgess. Three seasons later, the Phillies and Reds entered into a three-for-three trade, returning Seminick and Burgess to their previous teams.

At the time, Seminick was 34 and coming to the end of the line. He appeared in 93 games for the Phillies in 1955, in 60 games in 1956, and was then released. Apparently, it was hard for Seminick and the Phillies to say good-bye. They re-signed him on September 1, 1957, using him in eight games before releasing him once more.

Once again, it wasn't good-bye. The Phillies added Seminick to their coaching staff in 1957, and he remained an employee of the Phillies for the remainder of his career, serving for some four decades as a major-league coach, scout, roving minor-league instructor, and a minor-league manager during which time he coached or managed 90 players who eventually got to the major leagues, among them Hall of Famers Mike Schmidt and Ferguson Jenkins as well as Greg Luzinski and Bob Boone.

The guy whose defensive skills were said to be "below average" was credited with taking Boone under his wing and helping to convert him from a third baseman to a catcher who made four All-Star teams, won seven Gold Gloves, and had caught a record 2,225 games when he retired.

Had he not had knee injuries in the prime of his career, **Darren Daulton** might have been regarded as the greatest catcher in Phillies history and maybe even made the Hall of Fame. That's how good, and how productive, he was.

Darren Daulton (right) congratulates pitcher Curt Schilling after closing out a victory in Game 5 of the 1993 World Series.

Daulton was a late bloomer. He was 30 years old and in his ninth big-league season in 1992 when he exploded with 27 home runs, a league-leading 109 RBIs, and finished in the top 10 in the National League in on-base percentage, slugging percentage, OPS, home runs, walks, runs created, and extra-base hits. It earned him his first of three All-Star selections, a Silver Slugger Award (presented to the player who is the leading hitter at his position), and sixth place in the NL MVP voting.

He followed that up the next season with 24 homers, 105 RBIs, 117 walks, a second All-Star selection, and seventh place in the MVP voting—all while leading the Phillies to their first pennant in 10 years and being called "the greatest clubhouse leader the Phillies ever had."

He seemed on his way to baseball immortality when injury hit midway through the 1994 season. After 67 games, he was batting .300 with 15 home runs and 56 RBIs and a slugging percentage of .549 when he was felled by injury.

When he returned in 1996, his catching days were over. He would spend the remainder of his career as an outfielder, first baseman, and pinch-hitter.

Here's a quickie trivia quiz for you Philadelphia Phillies baseball buffs: Who caught the most games in Phillies history?

Over the next three seasons, he would play in only 187 games, hit 20 home runs, drive in 97 runs, and be traded to the Florida Marlins.

With the Marlins in 1997, he appeared in 52 games, batted .262, hit three home runs, and drove in 21 runs. But when the Marlins reached the World Series, Daulton turned it up a notch and showed his competitiveness. He appeared in all seven Series games against the Cleveland Indians, batting .389 with a home run and two RBIs. It would be his only World Series ring. It was a last hurrah for Daulton who, because of the condition of his knees, was forced to retire after the season.

Here's a quickie trivia quiz for you Philadelphia Phillies baseball buffs: Who caught the most games in Phillies history? Which catcher hit the most home runs as a Phillie? Who holds the team record for the highest fielding percentage as a catcher?

You win the prize if you answered Mike Lieberthal, Mike Lieberthal, and Mike Lieberthal.

That may surprise you. It did me; I would have guessed that Bob Boone, Andy Seminick, Stan Lopata, Darren Daulton, Clay Dalrymple, or Jimmie Wilson held those records. Certainly not **Mike Lieberthal**, who flew under the radar.

But Mike spent 14 seasons with the Phillies, from 1994 to 2006, and most of those years as their No. 1 catcher. He caught 1,139 games as a Phillie, hit all but one of his 150 home runs as a catcher, and posted a phenomenal .997 fielding percentage in 1999, which set a still-standing Phillies record for a catcher and won Lieberthal the Gold Glove. He also batted .300, hit 31 homers, and drove in 96 runs in what many believe was the greatest season for any Phillies catcher. He was only the eighth catcher to bat .300 and hit 30 home runs in the same season, and he joined Johnny Bench, Lance Parrish,

Mike Lieberthal is one of Philly's most unsung players at catcher.

and Ivan Rodriguez as the only catchers to hit 30 home runs and win a Gold Glove in the same year.

Lieberthal twice made the All-Star team, caught Kevin Millwood's no-hitter in 2003, and had a career fielding percentage of .991 and a career batting average of .274. Even so, he never got the credit he deserved, probably because in his 13 seasons with the Phils, they never made it to the post-season. Ironically, the Phillies won the National League pennant in 1993, the year before Lieberthal arrived, and won the National League East in 2007, the year after Lieberthal left.

As a 4'11" shortstop and second baseman, Mike was a high school star in Glendale, California, until his junior year when he switched to catcher at the urging of several professional scouts, including his father, Dennis, who at the time was a scout for the Detroit Tigers.

When he graduated in 1990, he had beefed up to 155 pounds and sprouted to almost 6'0" and was drafted by the Phillies in the first round, third overall, behind just Chipper Jones and Tony Clark and ahead of such future stars as Mike Mussina, Rondell White, and Garret Anderson.

In 2007 Lieberthal signed a one-year, $1.15 million free-agent contract with the Dodgers with a club option for 2008, but a series of injuries to his ankle, knee, and elbow limited Mike to just 38 games. Instead of picking up their option, the Dodgers exercised their $100,000 buyout and Lieberthal's career was over. But first, he signed a one-day contract with the Phillies so that he could retire as a Phillie.

Since his retirement from baseball, Lieberthal has devoted himself to charitable works, including Lieby's VIPs, which aids children with cancer and their families, serving as the 2000 chairman of a fund-raising drive for Corporate Alliance for Drug Education.

I thought I was all set with Smoky Burgess as the fifth-best catcher in Phillies history, but the longer I spent around the Phillies and the more I talked to their pitchers about him, the more I became enamored with Carlos Ruiz. And that has caused me to alter my thinking and make **Smoky Burgess and Carlos Ruiz** a double entry in the No. 5 slot.

The Phillies pitchers just love pitching to Ruiz. To a man, they all have told me that they never have to shake him off. I mean *never*! When you hear things like that from successful veteran pitchers such as Roy Halladay, Cliff

Carlos Ruiz is a homegrown star behind the plate.

Lee, Roy Oswalt, and Brad Lidge, that's impressive. It makes you sit up and take notice.

The interesting thing is that while Ruiz was coming up through the Phillies farm system, nobody in the organization doubted that he would hit—he batted .284 with 17 homers and 50 RBIs in 101 games at Reading in 2004, .300 at Scranton–Wilkes Barre in 2005, and .307 with 16 homers and 69 RBIs in 100 games with Scranton–Wilkes Barre in 2006—but there were questions about his defense. The skeptics needn't have worried. With the Phillies in 2007, he caught 111 games and committed only two errors in 744 chances, posting a fielding percentage of .997. What's more, he continued to hit—.259 with six home runs and 54 RBIs. The accolades earned him a spot on the Topps Rookie All-Star team.

Smoky stayed around as an effective, reliable, lethal, and cucumber-cool pinch-hitter a decade before the arrival of the designated hitter.

Ruiz has continued to improve on defense—one major-league scout called him "the best catcher in the game other than [the Minnesota Twins'] Joe Mauer, who's on a different planet"—and he's continued to hit, too. In fact, Ruiz has won over the demanding Phillies fans with his ability to hit in the clutch, producing some memorable big hits. For example, a bases-loaded infield single in the bottom of the ninth gave the Phillies a 5–4 win over the Tampa Bay Rays in Game 3 of the 2008 World Series, and a game-winning two-run double in the bottom of the ninth inning against the Dodgers gave the Phillies a 10–9 victory against L.A. in 2010 after they trailed 9–2 going into the eighth.

12

I wasn't able to find anyone who could satisfactorily explain why the Phillies acquired Smoky Burgess from the Reds in a trade for Andy Seminick and then three years later traded Burgess back to the Reds for Seminick.

What I do know is that while he was with the Phillies, Forrest Harrill Burgess put up impressive enough numbers (averages of .296, .292, and .368), for me to put him on my list of all-time Phillies catchers, and the Phillies would have been wise to keep him.

After he left Philadelphia, Burgess went on to play 13 more seasons with the Reds, Pirates, and White Sox. At the end of his career he was considered by many experts to be the greatest pinch-hitter in baseball history.

You'd never think it to look at him. He's listed as 5'8", but I have to believe he cheated by two or three inches. And he had a potbelly that made him look like a beer-league softball player—but boy, could he hit.

In his early days, Burgess was a good catch-and-throw guy behind the plate, but it was his bat that kept him around for 18 major league seasons and 1,691 games, banging out 1,318 hits and being named to six All-Star teams. He was signed by the Cubs in 1944, traded to the Reds in October 1951, and then dealt to the Phillies two months later without ever having played a game for Cincinnati. In Philadelphia, Burgess platooned with Stan Lopata. A left-

Smoky Burgess spent the early years of his career with the Phils, but it was later with the Pittsburgh Pirates that he had his most productive seasons.

handed hitter, he had his best season in 1954 when he batted .368, hit four homers, and drove in 46 runs in 108 games, making the All-Star team for the first time.

When he could no longer do the job behind the plate, Smoky stayed around as an effective, reliable, lethal, and cucumber-cool pinch-hitter a decade before the arrival of the designated hitter. When he retired after the 1967 season, Burgess had accumulated 145 pinch-hits, a major-league record that stood for a dozen years before it was broken by Manny Mota.

Statistical Summaries

All statistics are for player's Phillies career only.

HITTING

G = Games

H = Hits

HR = Home runs

RBI = Runs batted in

SB = Stolen bases

BA = Batting average

Catcher	Years	G	H	HR	RBI	SB	BA
Bob Boone *Led NL catchers in assists (89) and runners caught stealing (54) as rookie in 1973*	1972–81	1,125	349	65	456	23	.259
Andy Seminick *Slammed two home runs in eighth inning vs. Cincinnati, 6/2/49*	1943–51, 1955–57	985	716	123	411	20	.244
Darren Daulton *Hit his final major league home run vs. Phillies at Veterans Stadium 9/27/97*	1983, 1985–87	1,109	858	134	587	48	.245

continued	Years	G	H	HR	RBI	SB	BA
Mike Lieberthal *Had his most career HRs (17) and RBIs (73) against Atlanta Braves*	1994–2006	1,174	1,137	150	609	8	.275
Carlos Ruiz *Batted .375 in 2008 World Series*	2006–11	619	495	36	231	11	.265
Smoky Burgess *Only one of his 16 career pinch-hit homers came with Phillies (5/31/54 vs. Dodgers)*	1952–55	327	332	15	139	7	.316

FIELDING

PO = Putouts

A = Assists

E = Errors

DP = Double plays

TC/G = Total chances divided by games played

FA = Fielding average

Catcher	PO	A	E	DP	TC/G	FA
Bob Boone	5,677	573	91	67	5.8	.986
Andy Seminick	3,020	418	104	54	4.3	.971
Darren Daulton	5,417	445	66	70	6.1	.989
Mike Lieberthal	7,693	479	69	61	7.2	.992
Carlos Ruiz	3,929	300	23	25	6.6	.995
Smoky Burgess	1,225	101	24	18	4.6	.982

TWO

First Baseman

After only six full major-league seasons, **Ryan Howard** is already the No. 1 first baseman in Phillies history.

Heck, he was the No. 1 first baseman in Phillies history in his *first* full major-league season. That was 2006, when Howard took the National League by storm, batting a healthy .313; blasting 58 home runs to lead the league and obliterate Mike Schmidt's single-season club record by 10; leading the league with 149 RBIs, third on the Phillies' all-time list; accumulating a league-leading 383 total bases; compiling a slugging percentage of .659 and an OPS of 1.084; and being voted National League Most Valuable Player.

I guess he didn't have time to sell hot dogs in the stands between at-bats.

By taking the MVP Award—by a healthy margin over Albert Pujols—Howard joined Cal Ripken Jr. as one of two players in baseball history to win Rookie of the Year and MVP in back-to-back seasons.

By today's standards, Ryan's rise up the baseball ladder was a slow one. Born in St. Louis, he was drafted by the Phillies out of Missouri State

1. Ryan Howard

2. Pete Rose

3. Dolph Camilli

4. Jim Thome

5. Eddie Waitkus

Ryan Howard is a key component in the Phillies' recent success.

University in the fifth round of the 2001 amateur draft, a bountiful crop that also included Joe Mauer, Mark Teixeira, David Wright, Mark Prior, and Casey Kotchman. Howard would spend five seasons in the minor leagues at most of the stops in the Phillies system—Batavia, Lakewood, Clearwater, Reading, and Scranton—before landing in Philadelphia to stay in 2005 at the age of 25.

In only 88 games, he batted .288, hit 22 homers, and drove in 63 runs; he was the hands-down winner as National League Rookie of the Year.

Over the next six seasons, Howard established himself as one of the elite power hitters in Major League Baseball. In that six-year span he won three RBI titles and two home-run championships, hit 262 home runs (an average of 43.7 per year), drove in 796 runs (an average of 132.7 per year), became the first Phillie to knock in 100 or more runs in six consecutive seasons, and drew 505 walks, a sign of respect and fear from rival managers. At the same time he also struck out 1,094 times—and therein lies the rub.

Even the greatest players have flaws, and Ryan's are obvious. There's no denying he's a great player with awesome power, among the top two or three power hitters in the game. His numbers are Babe Ruth–like and it's not difficult to figure where his power comes from. He's a mountain of a man, 6'4" and over 240 pounds, with a violent left-handed swing. He has as much power to left field and left center as he does to right. No stadium can hold him. He can hit the ball out of any field—and some of the balls he's hit have been eye-popping. He's been on the receiving end of my "Cadillac time" call many times.

Ryan's power numbers speak for themselves and place him in the upper echelon of major-league power hitters.

The only negatives in Ryan's game are that maybe he strikes out a little too much and doesn't play as good a defensive first base as he could. For me, Ryan has to know the strike zone better. He has a tendency to chase pitches out of the zone, especially pitches in the dirt. If he learned to lay off those low pitches, pitchers wouldn't be able to get him out.

Just think, in his first big-league season, Howard batted .313. What that tells me is that he was swinging at strikes that year. Since then his average has dropped to .268, .251, .279, .276, and .253, respectively. He's still getting his home runs because he has that awesome power and he's going to run into a home run every once in a while just by accident. But pitches are getting him out because he's not swinging at strikes.

The Phillies have learned to live with the strikeouts because of the home runs and RBIs. Ryan's power numbers speak for themselves and place him in the upper echelon of major-league power hitters as well as at No. 1 all-time among Phillies first basemen.

And those numbers are amazing. He's already first on the Phillies' all-time list in slugging percentage, second to Mike Schmidt in home runs, and in the top 10 in RBIs with a bullet—ascending fast. But he's also third in strikeouts and is certain to overtake Schmidt for the top spot in a few years.

On top of everything, Ryan has been a good citizen and an active participant in community relations with his Howard Family Foundation and other charitable organizations that help disadvantaged youth and promote juvenile athletics in the Philadelphia area.

I realize the numbers may make it hard to justify selecting **Pete Rose** as the No. 2 first baseman in Phillies history. He was nearing the end of his fabulous career when he became a Phil, and he played for the team for only five seasons. What's more, in those five seasons he produced only eight home runs and 255 RBIs playing in what is traditionally a power position.

But he is, after all, Pete Rose. The irrepressible Pete Rose!

What Pete brought with him to Philadelphia was an impressive résumé; a reputation for fierce, relentless competitiveness; leadership; a winning attitude; a swagger, a cockiness, a passion, and a fire; and an enormous on-the-field ego—all the things a team needs in this game in order to be successful. All of that propelled the Phillies to two division titles, two National League pennants—including their first in 30 years—and the first World Series championship in their history.

I witnessed all of those qualities firsthand when I was Pete's teammate with the Phillies in 1981, '82, and '83. He was unique. And he was driven. If he had three hits in a game, he wanted four. If he had four hits, he wanted five. That's what drove him to break Ty Cobb's record and become baseball's all-time hits leader.

Pete was one of those players who got the most out of his ability. He may have gotten more out of his ability than anyone who ever played the game because he was not big, he was not fast, he wasn't a great defender, and he didn't have the sort of power that shrunk ballparks. But he was 100 percent baseball player.

Mainly, to me, Pete was a great teammate. He was a winner at any cost and the type of teammate to whom it didn't matter who you were, how big you were, what you were doing, whether you were a pitcher, or whatever. If he thought you weren't doing the job, he didn't mind getting on you. He'd get on you to get you to do better. And he wouldn't pull any punches.

Once when I was struggling, he said to me, "Hey, man, are you ever going to get another big hit for us this season?" The little shit! He'll say it at a time when you're struggling, down in the dumps, and on your last nerve. But he was never afraid to speak his mind. He did it as a player and he did it when he became a manager.

Back in those days, if someone—especially someone with Rose's résumé—got on you for something you didn't do, or if he seemed to doubt your ability, you wanted to make him eat his words. It motivated you.

It's beyond shameful that Pete Rose is not in the National Baseball Hall of Fame.

In 1983 the Phillies acquired Joe Morgan from the Giants in a trade and signed Tony Perez as a free agent. With that, the Big Red Machine was at it again. Perez got some big hits, and Morgan had a great month to help us win the NL East. Here was this little guy, 39 years old, putting the team on his back and carrying us to the playoffs. That year Rose proved that he was more than a pretty face and a hit machine. I found out in Game 3 of the World Series against the Baltimore Orioles that Pete also was a keen student of the game.

Pete Rose is on the outside looking in. That, to me, is a shame and an injustice.

Pete didn't have one of his better seasons in 1983, and for the World Series he was replaced at first base by Perez. Pete didn't complain about being benched, and he didn't brood. We had split the first two games and I remember going up to the plate against Mike Flanagan in the bottom of the second inning of Game 3. Pete told me to look first-pitch fastball. I did, and I hit the ball out of the park. I give Rose complete credit for that home run. It shows that even when he wasn't playing, he always was in the game.

It's unfortunate that he had to go through what he did, getting banned from baseball and excluded from the Hall of Fame, where I believe he belongs (his name has never even appeared on the ballot). With all the problems baseball has had with the apparent rampant use of steroids, to me it's a crying shame that Rose is left off the ballot and out of the Hall of Fame yet some of those steroid cheats (I'm talking about all those who have been charged with or admitted to taking steroids and other performance-enhancing drugs) *have* had their names on the ballot and might be rewarded by being elected to the Hall of Fame.

One of my good friends, Ryne Sandberg, had the courage to speak out and say that Sammy Sosa doesn't deserve to be in the Hall of Fame, period. And the late Bob Feller, right up to his death, carried the torch in support of guys who played without the benefit of steroids, human growth hormones, and other banned substances and artificial aids.

Feller and other old-time players understood how hard it is to be able to do the things you need to do to be a successful major-league player and took the position that players in the '60s, '70s, and '80s were justified in their use of amphetamines as a means of fighting off their lethargy from staying up late, drinking, and otherwise abusing their bodies. But, they argued, amphetamines don't enhance eye-hand coordination or make you stronger; they merely give you energy when you are dragging. That's a lot different than taking steroids that turn players into Incredible Hulks. All of a sudden players who never hit more than 20 home runs in a season were bulking up and hitting 50. And some of those guys may be elected to the Hall of Fame! But Pete Rose, who never hit 50 home runs in a season, never even hit 17 in a season, is on the outside looking in. That, to me, is a shame and an injustice.

Rose was a Phillie for only five seasons, but in those five seasons, he collected 826 of his record 4,256 hits, an average of 165 hits a season (including the strike year), batted over .300 for the 14th and 15th times in his career, collected at least 200 hits in a season for the 10th time, led the league in hits for the seventh time, and most importantly, taught his teammates how to win. And he did all of while playing from age 38 to 42.

The trade that brought first baseman **Dolph Camilli** to Philadelphia might have been the best the Phillies ever made. And the trade that sent Dolph Camilli away might have been their worst.

Camilli was born in San Francisco shortly after the turn of the 20th century, a time and a place that produced so many great baseball stars. (Do the names Joe and Dom DiMaggio, Tony Lazzeri, Lefty O'Doul, and Lefty Gomez ring a bell?)

Signed out of high school by the Cubs, Camilli would spend eight years in the minor leagues before finally reaching the majors.

In 1930, while Camilli was working his way up the ladder in the minor leagues, his older brother (by almost three years), fighting under the name Frankie Campbell, was killed in a San Francisco boxing ring by future heavyweight champion of the world Max Baer. The elder Camilli was 26 years old and a promising fighter who, with a record of 33–4—including 26 knockouts—was predicted to be on the fast track to a shot at the heavyweight title. The brothers were very close. Frankie cared for his younger sibling, and the two teenage brothers practically raised themselves after fleeing home to get away from an abusive father. Mercifully, on the night of August 25, 1930, Dolph was off playing for the Sacramento Senators of the Pacific Coast League and did not attend the fight. He was nonetheless devastated by the tragic loss of his big brother and best friend.

Dolph persevered and reached the majors with the Cubs in 1933, but after two rather pedestrian seasons he was traded midseason to the Phillies for first baseman Don Hurst.

Dolph Camilli makes a flying catch during Phillies spring training. *Courtesy of Getty Images*

At the time, the Phillies' owners were struggling desperately to keep the team from folding. To do so, they were forced to sell or trade their biggest stars, a veritable All-Star team including Chuck Klein, Pinky Whitney, Bucky Walters, Claude Passeau, Dick Bartell, Kirby Higbe, Spud and Curt Davis, and, eventually, Camilli himself. To appease their disgruntled fans, the owners emphasized that it was better to lose a player or two than to lose the entire team.

When Hurst batted .339 in 1932, hit 24 homers, and led the National League with 143 RBIs, the Phillies' owners knew they could not afford to keep him much longer. A year and a half later, Hurst was on his way to the Cubs and Camilli was coming to Philadelphia.

In Philly, Camilli became a star, batting .265, .261, .315, and .339 over the next four seasons while belting 92 homers and driving in 333 runs—in other words, pricing himself out of Philadelphia. The trade came on March 6, 1938, when the Phillies sent Camilli to the Brooklyn Dodgers for Eddie Morgan and $45,000, the 45G no doubt being more appealing to the Phillies' owners than the journeyman Morgan who would never play a regular-season game in a Phillies uniform.

Camilli helped turn around the fortunes of the Dodgers, who soared from seventh place in 1938 to third place, second, first, and second, respectively, over the next four seasons. In 1941 Camilli helped the Dodgers win their first pennant in 21 years when he led the league in home runs with 34 and RBIs with 120 and was voted National League Most Valuable Player. In a five-year stretch with the Dodgers, Camilli blasted 133 homers, an average of more than 26 per season, and drove in 529 runs, or 106 per year.

One can only conjecture what Camilli's potent bat might have meant to the Phillies, or if he would have put up such impressive numbers that Ryan Howard would still be chasing him for the spot of all-time Phillies first baseman.

It took only three seasons for **Jim Thome** to make enough of an impression to be included on my all-time Phillies team. Thome left when injuries and elbow surgery cut short his 2005 season, but seven years and 174 home runs later, he was back at the age of 41.

Thome had first come to the Phillies as a free agent in 2003 after spending 12 seasons with the Cleveland Indians. He had been drafted right out of high school as a third baseman by the Indians in the 13th round of the 1989 amateur draft. When the Indians acquired the veteran Matt Williams to play third base in 1997, Thome was moved across the diamond to first.

In Cleveland, Thome came under the tutelage of Charlie Manuel, first as his hitting coach (1994–99) and then as his manager (2000–02), and his career flourished as one of the American League's most damaging sluggers. Three times he hit 40 home runs or more and six times he drove in more than 100 runs in a season.

In Philadelphia, Thome was reunited with Charlie Manuel, who no doubt had some input in the Phillies signing the player. I personally know how much respect Charlie has for Thome. I've heard Charlie say that Thome is one of the best hitters he's ever been around.

In a 2007 poll of almost 500 major-league players, Jim Thome was voted by his peers, in a tie with Mike Sweeney, as the majors' second friendliest player. So it was not surprising that teammates and opponents alike were quick to add their congratulations on the occasion of Thome joining baseball's exclusive 600 Home Run Club.

"I was happy for him," said Derek Jeter, just days after joining an exclusive club of his own: the 3,000-Hit Club. "That's quite an accomplishment, 600 home runs. Jim is one of the nicest guys you'll meet in baseball. I've played against him for what seems like forever. It's something he should be extremely proud of. You can't say enough good things about him as a person. He's a great player and a good guy."

"Very rarely do you find a player where 100 percent of the people are pulling for him," said Phillies general manager Ruben Amaro Jr. "But I don't think there's anybody he's touched in baseball—and there's a lot of them—[who] wouldn't be pulling for Jim Thome."

Joe Nathan first faced Thome back in 2003 when Nathan was with the Giants and Thome was with the Phillies. Almost a decade later, they were teammates in Minnesota when Thome reached the 600-home-run plateau.

"Often you hear so much about some player on another team being such a great guy, and then when you get to know him, you're disappointed," said Nathan. "Not in Jim's case. You hear how much of a gentleman he is, how nice he is, and then you meet him and he's so nice, it's almost as if it's not real. You think nobody can be that nice. But Jim is... You realize it the moment you talk to him for the first time. He reminds me of Harmon Killebrew in the [sense] that you meet him for the first time and you know right away how genuine he is... It doesn't take you long to figure it out. Just like Harmon. There's no greater praise I can give anybody."

"On the field, Jim brings with him professionalism on a daily basis. He never gives away at-bats. He's going to give you a tough at-bat every time. That's something he passes on to young hitters who can learn just by observing him. He might strike out on three pitches, but he's going to be hacking on all three, and [everyone in] the whole ballpark will be holding their breath," Nathan continued.

"Obviously Jim is one of the greatest home run hitters of all time, so anytime you get a chance to compete against a guy like that it changes the game just in the way you have to strategize, the way you go about not only pitching to him but in the way you pitch to the guys around him. Not only is he a good player, he makes the players around him better."

Shortly after Thome reached the 600-home-run plateau, he was traded by the Twins back to his Cleveland roots, which caused Nathan to wax nostalgic.

"I'm glad I had the opportunity to get to know him as more than an opponent," Nathan said. "Getting the chance to finally play with Jim and to learn firsthand what kind of person he is and to be a small piece of history is really special. Watching him play brought me back to being a fan, being a kid again, watching a guy you look up to so much that you root for him no matter what team he's on. I want nothing but the best for him. Even though he's not my teammate anymore, I'll be rooting for him to get the World Series ring he's never had—as long as it's not at our expense, of course."

"I know him just like he was my son," Manuel said. "I spent that much time with him. He's very dedicated. Everything he's done, he's a credit to the game. His attitude is off the charts. He's totally genuine and totally legit."

In his first two seasons with the Phillies, Thome hit 89 home runs, including a league-leading 47 in 2003. He hit the 400th home run of his career in Philadelphia's Citizens Bank Ballpark in the first inning against the Reds' Jose Acevedo on June 14, 2004.

Thome is a true baseball player, an old-school type of guy who looks for the fastball and adjusts to the breaking ball. During one game in Toronto, when I was coaching with the Blue Jays and Thome was with the Indians, Pat Hentgen was pitching for the Jays. The count went to 3–0, and Pat threw a change-up that Thome hit off the glass in the upper deck in center field.

Thome had signed a six-year, $85 million free-agent contract with the Phillies, but by 2005 he was beginning to get the same feeling the legendary

Negro League pitching star Satchel Paige once described when he said, "Don't look back; something might be gaining on you."

The "something" gaining on Thome was Ryan Howard, who was tearing it up in the minor leagues and was on the fast track to Philadelphia. It was clear that Howard was in the Phillies' sights as their first baseman of the future, and with no designated hitter in the National League, that meant Thome's days as a Phillie were numbered.

Thome became the 23rd player to reach the 500-home-run milestone, and of all things, [did it on] Jim Thome Bobble Head Doll Day.

Shortly after the end of the 2005 season, Thome's brief but productive tenure with the Phillies came to an end when he was traded to the Chicago White Sox. There he continued to hit home runs and reach impressive heights.

In an 17-year span from 1994 to 2011, he hit at least 20 home runs in 16 seasons, missing out only in '05 when he was reduced to 59 games because of injury. On September 16, 2007, playing for the White Sox and with 25 family members and friends attending the game in Chicago's U.S. Cellular Field, Thome became the 23rd player to reach the 500-home-run milestone and embellished the event by making it a walk-off off the Angels' Dustin Moseley on, of all things, [did it on] Jim Thome Bobble Head Doll Day. It was the 12th walk-off home run of his illustrious career, tying him with Babe Ruth, Jimmie Foxx, Stan Musial, Mickey Mantle, and Frank Robinson for the most in baseball history.

But Jim Thome is not only about home runs and runs batted in. He's about being an all-around unselfish team player who, with all the homers and ribbies, also batted over .300 three times, collected 100 walks in a season nine times (leading his league three times), posted a higher career on base percentage than high-average Hall of Famers Tony Gwynn or Rod Carew, and scored more than 100 runs in a season eight times, as many times as Gwynn, Kirby Puckett, and Dave Winfield combined.

And Jim Thome is also about humanity. I hear that he's paying the tuition to send 10 of his nieces and nephews to college. That tells me that Jim is a special individual. It would be one thing to simply hand out $100,000 to your relatives, but to make certain they get an education tells me that his purpose is to see that his family gets the chance to grow and to know that the money he has earned is going to do some good for their future. It's no secret that the

Jim Thome (left) and Phillies great Mike Schmidt commemorate the last game at Veterans Stadium.

guys with the kind hearts and the guys who give back have a tendency to be elite players. There are exceptions to the rule, but his heart is why people pull for him. That's why he can go to different teams (the Indians, White Sox, Phillies, Dodgers, and Twins) and guys will say, "I can't believe what a great guy he is."

Mother Nature slows down everyone. As a player gets older, he's more susceptible to injury and recovery from those injuries takes longer. One knock on him is that since he left the National League, he has been used exclusively as a designated hitter. He's had back trouble that kept him from playing in the field, but he has continued to produce. He's a great person, and he's been a great teammate. He has courage. He makes other players around him better. He wants to win. He plays the game unselfishly, and he has played Major League Baseball for more than 20 years and he was still going strong and being productive in his forties.

You don't have to be a Hall of Famer to know a Hall of Famer, and to me Thome's numbers throughout his career demonstrate that when his time comes, he deserves to be a first-ballot Hall of Famer—and shame on those who don't vote for him.

It has long been a baseball truism that 500 home runs is an automatic ticket to Cooperstown. Because of the increase in home runs in recent years, some have revised that estimate and now say that 500 home runs no longer ensures Hall of Fame election. But on August 15, 2011, in Detroit, playing for the Minnesota Twins, Thome belted the 599th and 600th home runs of his career in consecutive at-bats. Now, as the eighth man to join the exclusive 600 Home Run Club, how are they going to keep Jim Thome out of Cooperstown?

Remember the famous scene in *The Natural*, based on Bernard Malamud's novel, when Roy Hobbs (played by Robert Redford) is shot by a crazed female fan?

Well, that actually happened to a major-leaguer named **Eddie Waitkus**, who makes my list of all-time Phillies first basemen at No. 5.

Until I checked him out and talked to some baseball people who have been around Philadelphia a long time, I knew nothing about Waitkus; I had never even heard his name. Even on first look, he wasn't very impressive.

After all, first base is supposed to be a power hitter's position. When you have a guy there who hit only 24 home runs, how can you be impressed?

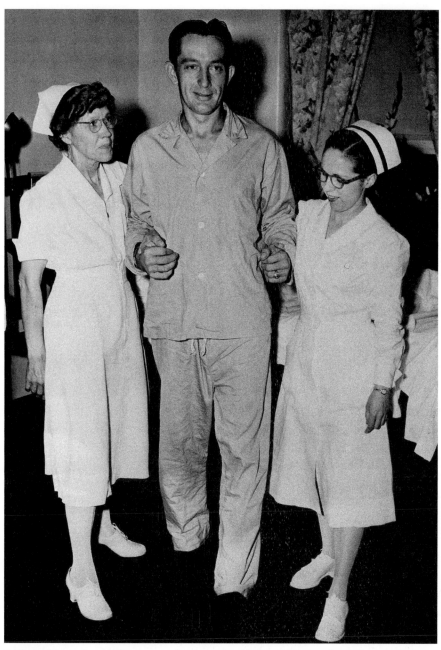

Eddie Waitkus takes his first steps after being hospitalized. He was shot by a crazed fan in 1949.

That's not 24 home runs in a season, mind you, it's 24 home runs in 11 seasons, 1,140 games and 4,254 at-bats, or an average of 2.18 home runs a season, one home run for every 47.5 games and one for every 177.25 at-bats. (By comparison, through 2011, Ryan Howard averaged 35.75 home runs per year and hit one for every 3.59 games and one for every 13.27 at bats). In those 11 seasons, 1,140 games, and 4,254 at-bats, Waitkus drove in only 373 runs.

To learn the real measure of Eddie Waitkus, you have to go beyond mere statistics. Born in Cambridge, Massachusetts, and educated at the prestigious Cambridge Latin High School and Boston College, Waitkus, the son of Lithuanian immigrants, spoke several languages fluently. He was signed by the Cubs in 1939 and moved quickly up the ladder in the Cubs' farm system. He had reached the Los Angeles Angels of the Pacific Coast League in 1942 when he was drafted into the U.S. Army. He served in the Philippines, where he was involved in heavy fighting and was awarded four Bronze Stars.

After the war, Waitkus returned to the Cubs in 1946 and made an immediate impact. Despite a lack of power, he was known as a slick-fielding first baseman with a career fielding percentage of .993, and was an excellent contact hitter. While batting .304, .292, and .295, but hitting only a total of 13 home runs in three seasons, Waitkus struck out only 50 times in 1,640 plate appearances and was named to the 1948 National League All-Star team.

After the 1948 season, Waitkus was traded to the Phillies. On June 14, 1949, Waitkus was batting .306 and had been named to the National League All-Star team for the game to be played a month later when the Phillies traveled to Chicago to begin a four-game series against the Cubs. When he checked into the Edgewater Beach Hotel, there was a note waiting for Waitkus summoning him to a certain room on an urgent matter. When he arrived, Waitkus was shot in the chest by an obsessed fan, Ruth Ann Steinhagen, who had been infatuated with him since his days with the Cubs.

The bullet just missed Waitkus' heart and he almost succumbed several times on the operating table during the removal of the bullet. Steinhagen never stood trial for the shooting, but instead was confined to a mental institution.

Waitkus returned to the Phillies in 1950, batted .284, drove in 44 runs, and played in 154 games and helped the Phillies win their first pennant in 35 years.

Statistical Summaries

All statistics are for player's Phillies career only.

HITTING

G = Games
H = Hits
HR = Home runs
RBI = Runs batted in
SB = Stolen bases
BA = Batting average

First Baseman	Years	G	H	HR	RBI	SB	BA
Ryan Howard *Had .400 lifetime average against John Smoltz and hit .385 against Greg Maddux*	2004–11	1,027	1,043	286	864	12	.275
Pete Rose *Finished second in batting race as Phillie in both 1979 and 1981*	1979–83	745	826	8	255	51	.291
Dolph Camilli *Led NL first basemen in putouts in both 1935 and 1936*	1934–37	540	585	92	333	23	.295

continued	Years	G	H	HR	RBI	SB	BA
Jim Thome *Hit .266 with 23 homers in first half of 2003 season and .267 with 24 homers in second half*	2003–05	361	333	96	266	0	.260
Eddie Waitkus *Had eight consecutive hits in doubleheader at Chicago, 8/27/50*	1949–53, 1955	613	649	9	197	9	.281

FIELDING

PO = Putouts

A = Assists

E = Errors

DP = Double plays

TC/G = Total chances divided by games played

FA = Fielding average

First Baseman	PO	A	E	DP	TC/G	FA
Ryan Howard	8,586	565	87	789	9.2	.991
Pete Rose	5,994	498	34	417	9.3	.995
Dolf Camilli	5,026	329	60	421	10.0	.989
Jim Thome	2,868	200	12	271	9.0	.996
Eddie Waitkus	5,054	382	42	529	9.3	.992

THREE

Second Baseman

I can't say enough about **Chase Utley**, as a player, as a leader, and as a competitor. I can lavish no higher praise on Utley than to say that he could have played in any era. Without a doubt he could have played in my era, or he could have played in the Negro League. In my mind, that's as good as it gets.

Utley is hardnosed. He plays the game the way it should be played. He's the ultimate competitor. You can't get him out twice in the same way in a game. To hit in the third slot on a team with so many great hitters, a team that has been a consistent powerhouse, says it all about Chase in a nutshell.

Signed by the Phillies out of UCLA as their first pick (15th overall) in the 2000 amateur draft, Utley moved seamlessly up the Phillies farm system from Batavia to Clearwater to Scranton/Wilkes-Barre.

Utley broke camp and traveled north with the big club in 2003 and on April 24 made his first major-league hit an especially memorable one: a grand slam off Aaron Cooke of the Colorado Rockies. However, after a about a month, Utley was sent back to

1. CHASE UTLEY

2. NAP LAJOIE

3. JUAN SAMUEL

4.-t TONY TAYLOR

4.-t COOKIE ROJAS

4.-t MANNY TRILLO

Chase Utley
is the ultimate
competitor.

36

Scranton/Wilkes-Barre, where he batted .323 with 18 home runs and 77 RBIs in 113 games. The Phillies realized what they had in Utley, a smooth-fielding, hardworking, dedicated left-handed–hitting second baseman with speed, great bat control, and power.

Despite all his tools, Utley created a dilemma for the Phillies, who were well protected at second base with Placido Polanco. At first, the Phillies tried a platoon situation, Polanco against left-handed pitchers, Utley against right-handers. But that was an ill-advised arrangement that benefited neither player nor the team. To break the logjam, Polanco was traded to the Detroit Tigers midway through the 2005 season, leaving Utley to handle second alone.

Utley was more than equal to the task. Beginning in 2005, he went on a streak of four consecutive seasons in which he batted no lower than .291, crashed no fewer than 22 home runs, and drove in no fewer than 102 runs. In 2006 he hit safely in 35 straight games, the second-longest hitting streak in Phillies history (Jimmy Rollins' 38-game streak is first) and tied Luis Castillo for the major leagues' longest hitting streak by a second baseman. The mark was also the longest hitting streak by a left-handed batter in 61 years; Tommy Holmes of the Boston Braves hit in 37 straight games in 1945.

In 2008 Utley joined Mike Schmidt, Dick Allen, and Bobby Abreu by hitting a home run in a Phillies franchise-record five consecutive games. Later that season, he received the ultimate compliment from the nation's First Fan when President George W. Bush, former owner of the Texas Rangers, said in an interview that if he were to start a baseball team, Utley would be the first non-pitcher he would select.

Later that year, Utley got some unwanted notoriety when, after the Phillies won the World Series, he was called to the microphone by announcer Harry Kalas and asked to address the crowd, and a large television audience, during a victory celebration at Citizens Bank Park. Caught up in the emotion and euphoria of the moment, and unaware that the broadcast did not have a tape delay, Chase uncharacteristically blurted an expletive that went out over the airwaves.

Utley's four-year run of more than 100 RBIs ended in 2009 when he drove in just 93, but another streak remained intact when the Phillies reached the World Series. Once again Chase Utley would add his name to the history books. In Game 1 of the Series at Yankee Stadium, Chase walked in the first inning, thereby setting a major-league record by reaching base in 26 consecutive postseason games. In his next two at-bats, Utley hit home runs off CC Sabathia, joining the mighty Babe Ruth as the only two left-handed hitters ever to hit two home runs in a World Series game against a left-handed pitcher.

Utley was not done yet. Four days later, he hit another home run off Sabathia. A day after that, in Game 5, he hit two more home runs, his fourth and fifth, tying Reggie Jackson for the most home runs in a World Series.

Since 2007 the Phillies have finished first in the National League East every year, and won two pennants and one World Series championship. And with Utley, a key member of the Phillies, still in his early thirties, there is every reason to expect that run of success to continue.

37

I don't personally know anything about **Napoleon Lajoie**, my choice as the second-best second baseman in Phillies history, and I don't know anyone who does, either. But he's in the Hall of Fame and that's good enough for me because I have great respect for the Baseball Hall of Fame in Cooperstown and anyone in it.

I obviously never saw Lajoie play (his last game was 34 years before I was born and he died when I was nine years old) so I have no way of knowing if he was a good fielder. But I believe in statistics, and when I look over Lajoie's numbers and see all those averages in the .360s, .370s, and .380s—and even one at .426—I can't help but be impressed.

I don't care when or where you do it—when you bat .426 for a season, you have to be something special.

I don't care when or where you do it—when you bat .426 for a season, whether it's in Little League or the major leagues, you have to be something special. And Napoleon Lajoie was something special, one of the magic names (how many people do you know named Napoleon?) in baseball's formative years.

Lajoie came out of Woonsocket, Rhode Island, and began his pro career with Fall River in the New England League, where he batted .429 in 80 games and caught the attention of the Philadelphia Phillies, who purchased his contract for $1,500. Lajoie spent five seasons with the Phillies, never batting below .324 and rivaling Pittsburgh's Honus Wagner as the National League's greatest player.

When National League owners implemented a salary cap of $2,400 per year for each player, Lajoie rebelled by jumping across town to the newly formed American League's Philadelphia Athletics, owned by Benjamin Shibe, a former part-owner of the Phillies, and managed by Connie Mack. In the new league's first season, in 1901, Lajoie led the American League in runs (145), hits (232), doubles (48), home runs (14), RBIs (125), total bases (350), batting average (.426), on-base percentage (.463), slugging percentage (.643), and OPS (1.106). So feared as a hitter was Lajoie that he became the second major-league player in history who was walked intentionally with the bases loaded. It has since been done four more times, including Barry Bonds in 1998 and Josh Hamilton in 2008.

The following year the Phillies obtained an injunction barring Lajoie from playing for any Philadelphia team besides the Phillies, thereby forcing the Athletics to sell him to the troubled Cleveland Bluebirds. Lajoie spent 13

Nap Lajoie was so popular in his day that they named an entire team after him.

seasons in Cleveland and saved the franchise while engaging in a rivalry for American League player supremacy with Ty Cobb. Lajoie was such an enormous hero in Cleveland that the team's name was changed to the Naps, which it remained until they were renamed Indians in 1915, the year after Lajoie departed.

Lajoie finished out his career in Philadelphia with the Athletics in 1915 and 1916. He retired with a lifetime batting average of .338, 3,242 hits, and his name sprinkled all over the American League offensive leaderboards.

When the Hall of Fame was created in 1936, five players—Ty Cobb, Babe Ruth, Honus Wagner, Christy Mathewson, and Walter Johnson—received the required 75 percent needed for election and comprised the charter members of the Hall. Lajoie finished sixth in the voting with 64.6 percent. The following year, however, he received 83.6 percent and was enshrined in Cooperstown along with Tris Speaker.

My first two choices for the five greatest second basemen in Philadelphia Phillies history, Chase Utley and Napoleon Lajoie, are on opposite ends of the chronological spectrum, having played as Phillies more than a century apart. Their selection was easy. The remainder is not.

The Phillies have had a collection of outstanding second basemen in a 40-plus-year span from the 1960s up to Utley's arrival in 2005, but there is no clear-cut choice for the final three spots. I have narrowed the selection down to seven players, Tony Taylor and Cookie Rojas from Cuba, Manny Trillo from Venezuela, Juan Samuel from the Dominican Republic, Marlon Anderson from Alabama, Dave Cash from New York State, and Mickey Morandini from Pennsylvania.

You can throw a blanket over all seven of them, so close are they statistically—especially when you consider their entire career numbers. For example, Taylor had a lifetime batting average of .261, Rojas .263, Trillo .263, Samuel .259, Anderson 265, Cash .283 ,and Morandini .268. Taylor had 75 career homers and 598 RBIs, Rojas was 54–593, Trillo 61–571, Samuel 161–703, Anderson 63–371, Cash 21–426, and Morandini 32–351.

Defensively, Taylor had a career fielding percentage of .976 and was involved in 950 double plays. Rojas was .984–953, Trillo .981–973, Samuel .973–630, Anderson .976–406, Cash .984–901, and Morandini .989–669.

So you can see how close they were, both at bat and in the field. It's almost as if the Phillies cloned their second basemen.

But remember, this is the Phillies all-time team, so I am almost (but not entirely) bound to make my choices based on how these individuals performed in the uniform of the Phillies. Also bear in mind that I believe statistics often tell only part of the story, and I'm more likely to go by my gut feeling than by the numbers, to put a higher premium on intangibles than on statistics.

I have such great respect for all seven of my second-base finalists, I'd like to vote a seven-way tie for the third, fourth, and fifth, but that would be the coward's way. I made a commitment to select the top five players at each position in order of preference (mine) and I will stick to that commitment, with one little hedge, a three-way tie for the final two spots. Regrettably, I must eliminate Anderson, Cash and Morandini (although he was the Phillies' starting second baseman for more seasons, eight, than anyone else in the team's history).

Juan Samuel was no slouch as a defensive second baseman, but in all honesty I'd have to rate Tony Taylor, Cookie Rojas, and Manny Trillo slightly ahead of him with the glove. Then why am I choosing Samuel ahead of the other three on my list, you ask? Easy! I am, and always have been, an

Dominican Republic native Juan Samuel coined the most famous phrase about the island country's baseball-rich tradition.

offensive guy. I like guys who can wreak havoc with the bat, do some damage, and dominate a game on offense—and Samuel has a big edge over the others in that department.

In his seven years with the Phillies, Samuel averaged 14.3 home runs and 59 RBIs per year, a decided advantage over Taylor (3.4 homers and 30.7 RBIs per year with the Phillies), Rojas (4.1 homers and 36.1 RBIs), and Trillo (4.8 homers and 40 RBIs).

Tony's arrival in Philadelphia was the result of one of the best trades the Phillies ever made.

Samuel came to the Phillies from San Pedro de Macoris, that lush municipality in the Dominican Republic that seems to grow baseball players on trees. For an area with a population of slightly more than 200,000, San Pedro de Macoris, often referred to as "the Cradle of Shortstops." has produced an inordinate number of major-leaguers (not only shortstops), among them Rico Carty, Pedro Guerrero, Sammy Sosa, Alfonso Soriano, Tony Fernandez, and Robinson Cano.

In his seven seasons in Philadelphia, Samuel put up some terrific numbers, the best of them in 1984, his first full season, when he batted .272, hit 15 homers, drove in 69 runs, hit 36 doubles, tied for the league lead in triples with 19, set a major-league rookie record with 72 stolen bases (broken the following season by Vince Coleman), and finished second to Dwight Gooden in the National League Rookie of the Year voting (though the *Sporting News* picked Samuel as its Rookie of the Year).

By 1987 Samuel had become the first player in major-league history to reach double figures in doubles, triples, home runs, and stolen bases in each of his first four seasons. He narrowly missed making it five straight seasons in 1988 when he hit just nine triples.

Samuel also is credited with a memorable quote about his homeland. Asked why Dominican batters are such notorious free swingers, he said, "You don't walk off the island, you hit your way off."

When his numbers began to slide at the end of the 1980s, the Phillies traded him to the Mets. Even then, Samuel made an indirect but huge contribution to the Phillies because the trade brought back center fielder Lenny Dykstra, a key component in the Phillies' 1993 pennant win.

Whether it was intentional or coincidental, I have to credit Juan with having a sense of humor by naming his son Samuel, making him, of course, Samuel Samuel.

Tony Taylor had three tours with the Phillies, the first as their regular second baseman, second as a valuable utility player and pinch-hitter, and the third as a coach. All told, he wore a Phillies uniform for 17 seasons and is one of the most popular players in Phillies history.

Tony's arrival in Philadelphia was the result of one of the best trades the Phillies ever made. They got him from the Cubs in 1960; he held down the second-base job for the next six seasons.

Taylor is fourth on the Phillies' all-time list with 1,669 games played, behind Mike Schmidt, Richie Ashburn, and Larry Bowa. He rates seventh in at-bats. He played in 1,003 games at second base for the Phillies, more than any other player except Utley, and is second on their all-time list in steals at home with six. He and Juan Samuel are the only two second basemen in the Phillies' Wall of Fame. Taylor and Cookie Rojas are two of only 40 players who have played all four infield positions for the Phillies.

Tony Taylor's numbers still stand on the Phillies' leaderboards.

Tony Taylor was replaced as the Phillies' starting second baseman in 1966 by **Cookie Rojas**, who had come over to Philadelphia three years earlier in a trade with the Cincinnati Reds. Rojas' father wanted him to be a doctor, but Cookie rejected his father's wish to pursue his passion for baseball. He signed with the Reds as a 17-year-old and moved up the ladder from Class A to the major leagues.

The Reds liked Rojas' defense, but they doubted if he ever would hit enough to be a top-flight major-leaguer, so they sent him to the Phillies in exchange for veteran relief pitcher Jim Owens. Rojas' hitting improved, and he spent four seasons as the Phillies regular second baseman, teaming with shortstop Bobby Wine to form a dazzling double-play combination. Soon, the media and fans began to rhapsodize about the double-play duo, referring to their exploits around second base as "the plays of Wine and Rojas," a takeoff on the song and movie, "The Days of Wine and Roses."

With a farmhand, Denny Doyle, making a strong bid to take over the Phillies' second-base job after the 1969 season, Rojas was included as part of a blockbuster trade that would turn out to be an important, critical, and historic event in baseball history. Rojas and Dick Allen were among a package of Phillies traded to the Cardinals for Tim McCarver, Joel Hoerner, and Curt Flood, the trade that would become the instrument leading to Flood's fight to challenge baseball's reserve clause and, eventually, to free agency and the multimillion-dollar contracts that would follow.

After only 23 games with the Cardinals, Rojas was traded to Kansas City, where he would become a mainstay with the Royals and a building block for a team that would win three American League East championships at the end of the 1970s.

They used to say about **Manny Trillo** that "nobody does it better," referring to his ability to turn the double play, the most important function of any second baseman.

Trillo was a magician at getting rid of the ball as the middleman on the double play if the throw from the third baseman or the shortstop or the pitcher hit him in the right spot. If the throw was errant, rather than risk losing both outs, he'd make sure to corral the ball and get the one sure out.

Trillo was a thinking man's second baseman. More than any other second baseman that I can think of, Manny would make a runner get lower sliding

44

Cookie Rojas was a media darling in his day. *Courtesy of Getty Images*

into second base to break up the double play. He did that by almost scraping his knuckles on the ground when he turned the ball over. His arm was so strong that he could get it over to first with a flick of the wrist better than any second baseman I've ever been around.

Offensively, Trillo was a line-drive hitter who was consistently around .260–.280 and between 50–60 RBIs throughout most of his career.

A key component in the Phillies' success was the play of second baseman Manny Trillo.

Manny was signed by the Phillies at 17 as a catcher and sent to Huron, South Dakota, in the short-season Northern League, where he had the good fortune to come across a young manager named Dallas Green, who converted him into a third baseman.

The Phillies lost Trillo to Oakland in the Rule 5 draft and he made it to the Athletics in 1973. Two years later, he was traded to the Cubs, where he became one of the best second basemen in the National League. In 1979, 11 years after he signed with them, Trillo was traded back to the Phillies. It was no coincidence that Manny's first pro manager, Dallas Green, was working in the Phillies front office as director of the minor leagues and no doubt had input on the trade.

A year later Green replaced Paul Owens as manager of the Phillies, and one year after that, Dallas led the Phils to their first World Series championship in franchise history. A key component in the Phillies' success was the play of second baseman Manny Trillo, who batted .292 with seven homers and 43 RBIs and had a fielding percentage of .987 during the regular season. He then batted .381 in the victory over Houston in the best-of-five NLCS for which he was voted Most Valuable Player.

In the World Series against Kansas City, with the Series tied at two and the Royals leading Game 5 3–2 in the sixth inning, Trillo threw out Darrell Porter at the plate as he tried to score on a double by Willie Wilson. Then, in the top of the ninth, Trillo singled home what would be the winning run in a 4–3 victory. The Phillies won Game 6, and the Series, at home.

Trillo would play nine more seasons with the Phillies, Indians, Expos, Giants, Cubs, and Reds and finish his career with 1,780 games, 1,562 hits, three Gold Gloves, two Silver Slugger Awards, four All-Star selections and a then-major-league record of 479 consecutive errorless chances at second base.

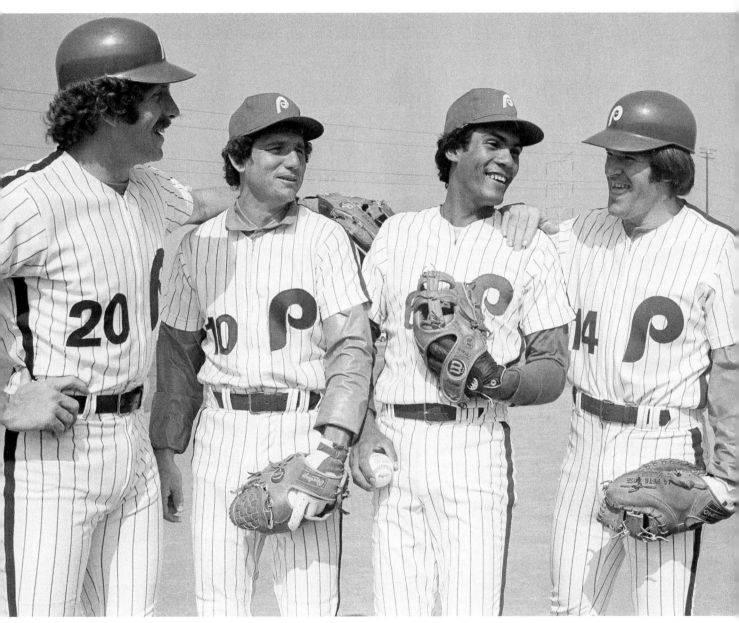

With the addition of Manny Trillo (second from right), the Phillies infield of (left to right)
Mike Schmidt, Larry Bowa, Trillo, and Pete Rose was poised for greatness in 1979.

Statistical Summaries

All statistics are for player's Phillies career only.

HITTING

G = Games

H = Hits

HR = Home runs

RBI = Runs batted in

SB = Stolen bases

BA = Batting average

Second Baseman	Years	G	H	HR	RBI	SB	BA
Chase Utley *.337 career average with bases loaded through 2011 season (31-for-92, 92 RBIs)*	2003–11	1,109	1,198	188	694	110	.290
Nap Lajoie *Finished in top three in NL in doubles, triples, and home runs in 1897*	1896–1900	492	721	32	458	87	.345
Juan Samuel *NL leader in at-bats three of four years from 1984 to 1987*	1983–89	852	921	100	413	249	.263

continued	Years	G	H	HR	RBI	SB	BA
Tony Taylor *13 hit-by-pitches led league in 1964*	1960–71, 1974–76	1,669	1,511	51	461	169	.261
Manny Trillo *Won the first two NL Silver Sluggers awarded at second base (1980–81)*	1979–82	502	516	19	160	30	.277
Cookie Rojas *Pitched a scoreless inning against San Francisco on 6/30/67*	1963–69	880	824	29	253	27	.262

FIELDING

PO = Putouts

A = Assists

E = Errors

DP = Double plays

TC/G = Total chances divided by games played

FA = Fielding average

Second Baseman	PO	A	E	DP	TC/G	FA
Chase Utley	2,237	2,895	91	665	5.0	.983
Nap Lajoie	953	983	98	158	6.5	.952
Juan Samuel	1,828	2,214	116	448	5.3	.972
Tony Taylor	2,206	2,558	115	630	4.9	.976
Manny Trillo	1,218	1,562	33	337	5.6	.988
Cookie Rojas	1,388	1,638	53	413	5.0	.983

FOUR

Shortstop

When you look at the resurgence of the Phillies in this millennium, it is not a stretch to say that it all began with the arrival of a little bitty infielder from Oakland, California, by the name of **James Calvin Rollins**, Jimmy to you, J-Roll to his friends and teammates.

Rollins was 17 years old, just a baby, when the Phillies drafted him and signed him out of high school in 1996. But he came with a reputation of excellence as a high school sensation and with an athletic pedigree. His mother was an outstanding player in fast-pitch softball, his brother played in the minor-league systems of the Texas Rangers and Montreal Expos, his sister was a starter on the University of San Francisco women's basketball team, and a cousin, Tony Tarasco, played eight major-league seasons with the Braves, Expos, Orioles, Yankees, Mets, and Reds.

1. JIMMY ROLLINS

2. LARRY BOWA

3. GRANNY HAMNER

4. DAVE BANCROFT

5. DICK BARTELL

Jimmy Rollins has outdone them all.

When Rollins got to the Phillies to stay in 2001 and took over as their shortstop, the team was in a state of flux. They had had only one winning

J-Roll is one of Philadelphia's most beloved players.

season in 14 years, and in that time they had six different shortstops. Jimmy would change all that and make his mark on the position.

It was Rollins' good fortune that when the Phillies handed him the starting shortstop job in '01, Larry Bowa had just taken over from Terry Francona as the team's manager. Bowa had been the Phillies' shortstop for 12 seasons in the 1970s and into the 1980s, and he was one of the best in the game a five-time All-Star. He took Rollins under his wing, nurtured him, tutored him, and helped J-Roll become the star player he is today.

Rollins made a positive impact from day one. He batted .274, led the league with 12 triples and 46 stolen bases, hit 14 homers, drove in 54 runs, played outstanding defense, made the All-Star team, helped the Phillies win 86 games and finish second in the NL East, and finished third to Albert Pujols and Roy Oswalt in the National League Rookie of the Year voting. Since Rollins arrived, the Phillies have had only one losing season, in 2002 (80–81). Though it was through no fault of Rollins. He led the league with 10 triples, hit 11 homers, drove in 60 runs, stole 31 bases, and again made the All-Star team, this time voted by fans as the National League's starting shortstop.

Over the next few years, Jimmy continued to put up impressive numbers, practically carrying the Phillies on his shoulders while at the same time developing into a team leader with energy, enthusiasm, baseball intellect, competitiveness, and durability. In his first seven full seasons, he would play in 1,100 of his team's 1,133 games (97 percent) and perform at an amazingly high level.

In 2005 he ended the season by hitting safely in his last 36 games, breaking the Phillies record set in 1899 by Ed Delahanty. He would run the streak to 38 by hitting safely in the first two games of 2006, set a team record for home runs by a shortstop with 25 (he would increase his record to 30 homers the following season), and team with Chase Utley (32) to become the first pair of middle infielders in National League history to hit at least 25 home runs in a season as teammates.

Talk about putting a team on your shoulders and making other players around you better: Rollins hit the motherlode in 2007, with 20 triples to lead the league in that category for the fourth time, 30 homers, 41 stolen bases, a .296 batting average in 162 games, and a remarkable 778 plate appearances. He was the fourth player in baseball history to have at least 20 doubles, 20 triples, 20 homers, and 20 stolen bases in the same season, all of which earned him National League MVP honors.

You may have noticed that Rollins, Utley, and Ryan Howard, my No. 1 picks at three of the four infield positions, all played with the Phillies at the same time. I doubt if the same could be said for any other major-league team. The three have been together in the Phillies infield in every season since 2005, and in that time the Phillies finished second in the National League East twice, and won the division title five times, the National League pennant twice, and the World Series once. That can hardly be considered a coincidence.

Larry Bowa was the Phillies' starting shortstop longer than any other player (12 consecutive seasons from 1970 to 1981) and played more games at shortstop for the Phillies than anybody else (1,739). Those two facts alone would be enough to include Bowa among the top five shortstops in Phillies history. Throw in two Gold Gloves, five All-Star selections, six times leading

53

National League shortstops in fielding percentage—five with the Phillies and one with the Cubs—and a handful of other major-league marks, all for defense, and you have an idea why I have him at No. 2 on my list.

Only Jimmy Rollins is rated higher among Phillies shortstops, and that's mainly because of his bat. Although Bowa was a pretty good switch-hitter (he batted over .300 once, .280 or higher four times and had a lifetime average of .260 through 16 seasons), he didn't produce runs like J-Roll; Bowa had only 15 career home runs and 525 RBIs in 2,247 games.

It's hard to believe that after all he accomplished, and considering he's the son of a former minor league infielder and manager in the Cardinals' farm system, that Bowa didn't even make his high school baseball team.

To his credit, after high school, Bowa, a native of Sacramento, worked hard and made himself into a player good enough to start for his hometown team, Sacramento City College but not good enough, according to most scouts, to waste a draft pick on him. Only the Phillies showed enough interest in Bowa to send a scout to Sacramento City College and watch Bowa play in a doubleheader. What the scout saw was the future Larry Bowa. He was tossed out of the first game for arguing with an umpire.

A five-time All-Star, Larry Bowa was one of the top shortstops in the 1970s. *Courtesy of Getty Images*

The scout ran an amateur winter league team and invited Bowa to play with his team. Larry accepted and impressed the scout/coach enough that the Phillies offered him a minor-league contract, which Bowa signed for a measly bonus of $2,000.

Bowa moved steadily up the Phillies ladder, from Spartanburg to Bakersfield to Reading to Eugene until 1970, when he was handed the starting shortstop job in Philadelphia. Prior to Bowa's arrival, the Phillies had used four different shortstops in four years and had not won a pennant in two full decades.

If Bowa's fiery temper caused him to burn bridges as a player, that same temperament attracted teams to him as a manager.

Flanked at third base by Mike Schmidt, Bowa was instrumental in turning the Phillies around, helping them win four division titles and make the playoffs five times in a six-year span, 1976–81.

It was at about that time that Bowa was beginning to wear out his welcome in Philadelphia. A trade was worked out with the Cubs, and Larry spent three seasons as the Cubs' starting shortstop, but lost his job to Shawon Dunston in 1985, which didn't sit well with Larry. He burned another bridge by blasting the Cubs, apparently hastening his release in August. A week later, he signed with the New York Mets but appeared in only 14 games with them before retiring.

When he left, he had played more games at shortstop than any other National Leaguer and held major-league records in career (.980) and season (.991) fielding. He was sixth all-time in assists and fourth in double plays.

If you're wondering why such a skillful shortstop didn't win more than two Gold Gloves, there are two reasons: Davey Concepcion won it in four straight years from 1974 to 1977 and again in 1979, and "the Wizard," Ozzie Smith, won it for 13 straight years, from 1980 to 1992.

If Bowa's fiery temper caused him to burn bridges as a player, that same temperament attracted teams to him as a manager. The San Diego Padres thought Bowa's demeanor could light a spark under a moribund franchise, but in a season and a half, Larry had won only 81 of 208 games and was fired.

Meanwhile, Bowa had mended his fences in Philadelphia. The Phillies installed him in their Wall of Fame in 1991, and 10 years later they brought him in to take over as manager for Terry Francona. Larry took a team that had finished in last place in the NL East and brought them home in second place, two games behind the leader, with a record of 86–76. The feat earned him National League Manager of the Year honors.

The Phillies finished in third place in each of the next two seasons and in 2004 they were in second place with two games remaining when Bowa was fired. His record at the time was 85–75, a winning percentage of .531, the exact same percentage as he had earned in his Manager of the Year season. However, instead of being two games off the lead, this time he was a well-beaten 10 games behind the Atlanta Braves, and the Phillies had Bowa's successor waiting in the wings, a fella named Charlie Manuel.

You can make a strong case for **Granny Hamner** as one of the Phillies' top five at either second base or shortstop. For two reasons, I chose to put him at shortstop:

1. Except for 27 games with Cleveland and three with the Kansas City Athletics at the end of his career, Hamner spent his entire career with the Phillies and played more games at shortstop (924) than at second base (561).
2. He was the shortstop and a key man for the 1950 Whiz Kids National League championship team, batting .270 with 11 home runs and 82 RBIs and leading his team with a .429 average in the four-game sweep by the Yankees in the World Series.

Granville Wilbur "Granny" Hamner signed with the Phillies out of high school in 1944 and got into 21 games that season without having played a game in the minor leagues. Many of the majors' top pitchers were off serving in the armed forces during World War II, and Hamner made an immediate impression by getting 19 hits in 77 at-bats, a .247 average. He was only 17 years old.

When Hamner's brother Garvin, three years Granny's senior, joined the team in 1945, the similarity in their names caused confusion among teammates, opponents, fans, sportswriters, and even major-league executives. The St. Louis Browns had scouted Granny and planned to select him in the Rule 5 draft off the roster of the Utica Blue Sox but selected Garvin by mistake; Granny remained with the Phillies.

When the Phillies opened the season in Brooklyn on April 17, the Hamner brothers made up their double-play combination, Garvin at second base, Granville at shortstop. Three days later, against the Boston Braves, they pulled off their first double play, Garvin to Granville to Wasdell.

A second baseman, shortstop, and even pitcher, Granny Hamner comes in No. 3 on my list of Phillies shortstops. *Courtesy of Getty Images*

Garvin's entire major-league career consisted of 32 games with the Phillies in 1945. He batted .198 and drove in five runs and spent the next eight years in the minor leagues, finally retiring after the 1953 season. Meanwhile, kid brother Granny had a stellar 17-year career in which he batted .262, hit 104 homers, and knocked in 708 runs.

A dependable clutch hitter and a natural leader, Hamner was so highly regarded that in 1952, manager Eddie Sawyer named him captain of the Phillies when he was just 24 years old. The added responsibility seemed to bring out the best in Hamner, as he had his finest seasons in 1952–54, batting .275, .276, and .299, respectively; hitting 51 homers; driving in 268 runs; and making the All-Star team all three years.

In 1959 Hamner was traded to the Indians, who released him after the season. Granny returned to the minor leagues, where he briefly managed in the Kansas City farm system and then reinvented himself as a pitcher. With the Phillies in 1956 and 1957, he had dabbled as a pitcher, appearing in four games. He believed he could pitch his way back to the major leagues.

He won 15 games in the minors over a three-year period and returned to the big leagues with the Athletics to pitch in three games in 1962 before calling it a career as a player.

Sadly, Hamner died in 1993 after watching the Phillies in a game against the Houston Astros but lived to see his plaque added to the Phillies Wall of Fame six years earlier.

It's a baseball old wives' tale that you can't win a pennant with a rookie short-stop. But nobody told that to **Dave Bancroft**, who, one can argue, was the difference-maker in the 1915 National League.

Until then, the Phillies had never won a pennant. In the previous six seasons, they had finished sixth, second, fifth, fourth, fourth and fifth. One can make the case that Bancroft, a 24-year-old rookie, was the missing ingredient that turned the Phillies from also-rans into champions.

Bancroft began his professional career at the age of 18 with the Duluth White Sox and Superior Blues in the Class D Minnesota-Wisconsin League. He moved up slowly—two years in Class D, one in Class C, one in Class B and, finally, two seasons with the Portland Beavers in the Class AA Pacific Coast League where the Phillies spotted him and purchased his contract for $5,000 just before the start of the 1915 season.

Davey Bancroft was inducted into the Hall of Fame on the "Beauty" of his defensive game.

Bancroft took over as the Phillies' starting shortstop two years after Mickey Doolan, who had capably manned the position for the Phillies for nine seasons before jumping to Baltimore in the rival and short-lived Federal League. Their new shortstop was a revelation for the Phillies, batting a respectable .254 with seven home runs, 30 runs batted in, and 15 stolen bases. Bancroft played excellent, often spectacular, defense, helping the Phillies win 90 games and finish first in the National League pennant race, seven games in front of the Brooklyn Robins (later renamed the Dodgers).

Bancroft's nickname was "Beauty," which had less to do with his handsome face and more to do with his grace and agility in the field.

Most observers agreed that the Phillies would not have reached the World Series without their rookie shortstop.

The following year, the Phillies actually improved their win total to 91, yet finished second to the Robins by 2½ games. When the Phillies began to decline they were forced to unload some of their top players in order to meet their financial obligations. Among those sacrificed was Bancroft, who was dealt to the New York Giants midway through the 1920 season for shortstop Art Fletcher, pitcher Bill "the Wrong" Hubbell, and a bundle of cash.

A sidenote: there was nothing similar between the two pitching Hubbells except their surnames. Bill, a right-hander from Henderson, Colorado, was six years older than Carl, a left-hander from Carthage, Missouri. Bill won 40 major-league games. Carl won 213 more games than his namesake and was elected to the Hall of Fame.

Bancroft's nickname was "Beauty," which had less to do with his handsome face and more to do with his grace and agility in the field. (Although it seems to be some kind of irony that when his major-league career ended, Bancroft managed the Chicago Colleens and South Bend Blue Sox in the All-American Girls Professional Baseball League.) As a player, it was with the Giants that Bancroft had his best seasons and made his greatest impact. In his three full seasons as a Giant, Bancroft batted .318, .321, and .304 and helped the Giants win three National League pennants and two World Series.

He retired in 1930 and had to wait 41 years to be admitted to the Hall of Fame, but at least he had the satisfaction of smelling the roses. He was enshrined in Cooperstown in 1971 and died a year later.

Obviously, I never saw Bancroft play and I don't know anyone who did, but reading and hearing about him made me think he was his era's Jimmy Rollins. Bancroft is listed in the record books as 5'9", 160 pounds. Rollins is 5'8", 170. Both are shortstops. Both are switch-hitters. And both were their team's catalyst.

There's a reason they called **Dick Bartell** "Rowdy Richard." He was a battler and a feisty, combative, and ferocious competitor who kept wearing out his welcome and getting traded away. He played for five teams—the Pirates, Phillies, Giants, Cubs, and Tigers—in his often spectacular 18-year career and produced with each club. But eventually he gave each of them a reason to get rid of him.

Bartell's journey began in Pittsburgh in 1927 after one minor-league season when the Pirates brought him up in September to play in one game. He was 19 years old, the youngest player in the National League.

The Pirates made Bartell their shortstop in 1928, choosing him over Joe Cronin, who would go on to a distinguished career as a Hall of Fame shortstop with the Boston Red Sox and later as president of the American League. Bartell rewarded the Pirates' faith in him with three outstanding seasons in which he batted .305, .302, and .320 while playing outstanding defense, making it curious why he was then traded. The reasonable conclusion to draw was that the Pirates wearied of Bartell's rowdiness.

Off he went with his aggressiveness, his productive bat, and his magic glove to Philadelphia, where he gave the Phillies four outstanding seasons. In Philly, he batted .289, .308, .271, and .310; twice scored more than 100 runs and hit more than 40 doubles; helped the Phillies finish in the first division of the eight-team National League for the only time in a 31-season span (1918–48); and was the NL's shortstop in the first All-Star Game in 1933.

Despite his success, after the '38 season, the Phillies cut ties with Bartell not so much for his rowdiness as to save the franchise during a period of financial woes by unloading such stars as Chuck Klein, Pinky Whitney, Dolph Camilli, Bucky Walters, Kirby Higbe, and Bartell, who was traded to the Giants for cash and four players including a blond and a pretzel. No, seriously! From the Giants, in return for Bartell, the Phillies received John "Blondy" Ryan and John "Pretzel" Pezzullo.

Diminutive Dick Bartell sits on the shoulders of Giants teammate Jumbo Brown in 1938. *Courtesy of Getty Images*

I don't want to overlook two Phillies shortstops, Ruben Amaro Sr. and Bobby Wine, who fail to make my top five because of a lack of offense, due largely to their careers being injury-plagued. Amaro and Wine were a couple of defensive wizards (before Ozzie Smith) and worthy of mention in any discussion of Phillies shortstops.

Amaro, the father of current Phillies general manager, Ruben Amaro Jr., was a smooth-as-glass fielder with amazing range who made some plays worthy of a highlight reel in an era (the 1960s) before there were such things as highlight reels.

Pretty much the same can be said of Wine, who won a Gold Glove in 1963, led National League shortstops in fielding in 1967, spent decades as a major-league coach and scout, and was forever immortalized by sportswriters writing about "the plays of Wine and Rojas."

Statistical Summaries

All statistics are for player's Phillies career only.

HITTING

G = Games
H = Hits
HR = Home runs
RBI = Runs batted in
SB = Stolen bases
BA = Batting average

Shortstop	Years	G	H	HR	RBI	SB	BA
Jimmy Rollins *Through 2011 has led off game with a home run 37 times*	2000–11	1,636	1,866	170	725	373	.272
Larry Bowa *Led NL shortstops in fielding percentage six times, five times as Phillie*	1970–81	1,739	1,798	13	421	288	.264
Granny Hamner *Tied Gene Woodling of Yankees for best batting average in 1950 World Series (.429)*	1944–59	1,501	1,518	103	705	35	.263

continued	Years	G	H	HR	RBI	SB	BA
Davey Bancroft *Went 6-for-6 against Phillies on 6/28/20, three weeks after being traded to Giants*	1915–20	681	634	14	162	64	.251
Dick Bartell *Slammed four doubles against Braves on 4/25/33*	1931–34	587	695	2	161	33	.295

FIELDING

PO = Putouts

A = Assists

E = Errors

DP = Double plays

TC/G = Total chances divided by games played

FA = Fielding average

Shortstop	PO	A	E	DP	TC/G	FA
Jimmy Rollins	2,217	4,503	112	939	4.2	.984
Larry Bowa	2,457	5,213	145	961	4.5	.981
Granny Hamner	1,561	2,798	247	569	5.0	.946
Davey Bancroft	1,655	2,357	270	308	6.4	.937
Dick Bartell	1,405	1,937	160	372	6.0	.954

FIVE

Third Baseman

This is the easiest selection I have had to make. Not only is **Mike Schmidt** the No. 1 third baseman in Phillies history, he's arguably the No. 1 *player* in Phillies history—a first-ballot Hall of Famer and in the minds of many, including me, the greatest third baseman ever to play the game.

We celebrate Schmidt for his bat: the 548 home runs, just ahead of Mickey Mantle; the 1,595 runs batted in, just ahead of Rogers Hornsby and Harmon Killebrew; the eight home-run championships; the four RBI titles; the six Silver Slugger Awards. We extol him for winning three MVP Awards and earning 12 All-Star selections.

But how about the 10 Gold Gloves? Among third basemen, only Brooks Robinson has won more.

As a player, Mike was the ultimate thinker, running the play through his head before it happened. If he was coming in to make a play, he might go home with it. If he backhanded the ball, he already knew if he was going to second or first, depending on who the runner was. There were times he

1. MIKE SCHMIDT

2. DICK ALLEN

3. SCOTT ROLEN

4. WILLIE JONES

5. PINKY WHITNEY

might catch a ball and fake a throw. He had it all planned out in his mind before the play, anticipating the various possibilities and what he would do if the ball came to him.

As a hitter, he would think along with the pitcher. He knew his strength at bat. Early in his career, he struck out a lot—467 times in the three seasons from 1974 to 1976, leading the league each year—but as he got older he was able to cut down on his strikeouts. By 1985 he struck out only 84 times in 645 plate appearances; in 1986, it was just 80 times in 613 plate appearances.

It seems that Schmidt was destined from an early age to be a baseball star. He grew up in an upper-middle-class family and, as a kid, he devoted his time to sports. He was a great bowler, was exposed to golf at an early age, and concentrated on baseball.

There is no set formula for success in sports. People are motivated to be great for different reasons. Some guys are motivated by hunger, a desire to excel in order to make something of themselves and improve their station in life. Those guys are hungry, and they love the game. To them, sports are a means of survival. Others, like Schmidt, grow up in a comfortable and secure environment that can help them grow as a person and as an athlete. It's a little bit different. Those guys are not hungry, they are not fighting to survive; they just love the game. They want to get to the top and that's what motivates them.

Back home in Dayton, Ohio, Schmidt was a star in Little League and so dominant that in 1991 he was voted into the Little League Hall of Excellence. After graduating from high school, Mike attended Ohio University and led his team to the 1970 College World Series. The following year, the Phillies made him their second-round pick, 30th overall, in baseball's amateur draft. Incidentally, George Brett was drafted just ahead of Schmidt, thus two of the 14 third basemen in the Hall of Fame were drafted back to back in 1971.

After half a season at Reading in the Class AA Eastern League and a full season at Eugene in the Triple A Pacific Coast League, in which he batted .291 with 26 homers and 91 RBIs, Schmidt was brought up to Philadelphia. There he batted a mere .196 and struck out 136 times in 132 games with the Phillies through the season. But team brass was nonetheless impressed with young Schmidt's 18 home runs and 52 RBIs.

The following year, Schmidt began a 14-year run in which he averaged 36.5 home runs and 103.6 RBIs per season, and won his three Most Valuable Player Awards, his eight home run and four RBI titles, and 10 Gold Gloves.

Mike Schmidt is the all-time Phillies great.

On April 17, 1976, Schmidt became the 10th player in baseball history to hit four home runs in a single game when he did it against the Cubs in Wrigley Field. Mike also helped the Phillies win three consecutive National League East crowns, in 1976–78, but each time they were defeated in the NLCS, once by the Reds and twice by the Dodgers. Then along came Pete Rose.

After falling back to fourth place with a record of 84–78 in 1979, the Phillies rebounded to win 91 games and finish first in the NL East. Schmidt batted .286, led the league with 48 homers and 121 RBIs, and won his first MVP Award. The Phillies then beat Houston in the NLCS, three games to two, and beat Kansas City to win their first World Series. Schmidt batted .381, hit two homers, knocked in seven runs, and was named Series MVP.

Why isn't [Dick] Allen in the Hall of Fame? Circumstances!

Although he batted only .261 against Kansas City, I believe it was Pete Rose who had a lot to do with the Phillies winning that World Series. He showed a lot of those guys on the Phillies how to win. And he was a big influence on Schmidt, helping him become the player he became, dealing with the daily grind and learning what it took to be a winner.

Schmidt was a great player, and he would have been a great player even if he never met Pete Rose, but I believe Rose still elevated Schmidt's game. Pete brought some swagger and some cockiness that players have to have to be successful in this game. He was a fierce competitor and he set an example for Schmidt to follow. Mike observed the way Pete would grind on a daily basis. That kind of stuff makes an impression. Watching Pete day after day made Schmidt an even fiercer competitor than he had been and, as a result, it made him a better player.

Rose was one of Schmidt's biggest boosters. He once said of Schmidt, "To have his body, I'd trade him mine and my wife's, and I'd throw in some cash."

Schmidt retired during the 1989 season having done what today is considered a rarity: playing his entire 18-year major-league season with one team. He retired leaving a legacy for all future Phillies to chase as the team's all-time leader in games played, at-bats, plate appearances, runs scored, hits, home runs, RBIs, walks, strikeouts, total bases, runs created, sacrifice flies, outs, extra-base hits, and times on base.

When you look at Mike Schmidt as an all-around player, the home runs, the RBIs, the Gold Gloves, the baseball instincts, the base running, the thinking man's approach to the game, the competitiveness—and being a major part of the team that won the first World Series in Phillies history—there's no doubt in my mind that outside of pitchers, Schmidt is easily the greatest player in Phillies history.

Dick Allen rates at or near the top of my list among all-time Phillies at either first base or third base. My first inclination was to include him among the first basemen because that's where I remember him playing most of the time. Then I realized I was thinking about the Dick Allen who played for the Cardinals, Dodgers, and White Sox, not the Dick Allen who started his major-league career with the Phillies. That Dick Allen (he was Richie Allen back then), played more games at third base (545) than he did at first base (315). Unfortunately, his record at third base does not distinguish him; for example in 1964, his rookie season, he played 162 games at third and made 41 errors.

But when you talk about Allen—especially when you talk to pitchers who faced him—you don't talk about defense, you talk about a guy who was one of the most feared hitters of all time, you talk about someone who hit such tremendous, tape-measure home runs that now, more than half a century later, people are still in awe of those shots in Philadelphia, St. Louis, and Chicago. You talk about a guy who should be in the Hall of Fame but isn't.

Why isn't [Dick] Allen in the Hall of Fame? Circumstances! At least, that's what I believe. Look at when he played, the 1960s and '70s, a time when there was much unrest and racial discord in this country. It was a lot to endure back then, playing in cities that don't necessarily want you there. Some players were able to accept it and succeed and some were not. Dick Allen was one who wouldn't accept it. He was the anti–Jackie Robinson.

Robinson was willing and able to accept the things he endured, the things he didn't like but knew he could not change overnight. That's why everybody says that Robinson was the right one to break baseball's color line. How many players would have been able to endure everything Jackie went through, from the name-calling to the death threats to not being able to go to the same hotels or restaurants as the other players. Robinson was a special person to have done that. Another man might not have been able to. Another man might have set the process back years, even decades.

Because of Robinson, things were better when Dick Allen came along, but they still were far from where they needed to be. Allen was not able to cope with it.

*F*ew major-leaguers have engendered as much passion as Dick Allen, a lightning rod who brought revulsion from some (fans and members of the media) and reverence from others (teammates). In that latter group falls Jim Kaat, who played 25 major league seasons with five different teams. In his long career, he had hundreds of teammates but counts Allen—his teammate with the White Sox in 1973–74 and the Phillies in 1976—among his handful of favorites.

"Dick had an adversarial relationship with the press, and when I found out I was going to be playing with him, I wondered what it was going to be like. It turned out to be a great experience," Kaat said.

"When I first got to Chicago, Dick was out with an ankle injury, and he missed quite a bit of time. But the next year we began bonding. We both liked horse racing and we both liked baseball. He had learned the game playing for Gene Mauch, and I found Dick to be a guy you could sit with and talk about the inside of the game, which I often did.

"Dick didn't care if he went 4-for-4 or 0-for-4; he was more interested in doing the little things you had to do to win the game. He could run the bases and play defense, and he could hit. Boy, could he hit!

"We got on well together. He liked that I worked fast, that I was into the game, and that I was always talking to my infielders. I'd say, 'Heads up, now, this may be coming your way.' Dick loved that. To this day he tells people the two pitchers he most enjoyed playing behind were Bob Gibson and me.

"Dick called me 'old timer' because I was the oldest guy on the team. [White Sox manager] Chuck Tanner used to let Dick have his way. On days when I was pitching, I would sit at my locker rubbing up the baseball, and a half hour before the game Dick would come sashaying in, and he'd see me and say, 'Hey, old timer, you pitching tonight?'

"'Yeah.

"'Good. We'll be out of here in an hour and 45 minutes,' he'd say.

"Dick had come to the White Sox in 1972, the year before I got there. The previous year the Sox had drawn a little more than 800,000 fans and finished four games under .500. Dick turned things around almost single-handedly. He batted .308, led the league with 37 homers and 113 RBIs and was the Most Valuable Player. He carried that team. The Sox drew almost 1.2 million fans, were 20 games over .500—a 24-game improvement over the previous year—and just missed catching the powerhouse Oakland team of Reggie Jackson, Sal Bando, Joe Rudi, Rollie Fingers, Catfish Hunter, and Vida Blue for first place in the American League West. They began calling him 'Mose' because like Moses, Allen almost led the White Sox to the Promised Land," Kaat continued.

"I had the good fortune to play with a few players I call legendary, such as Harmon Killebrew and Pete Rose. I put Dick Allen in that category. He was truly legendary. He always wore the hard hat, even in the field. He would sit in the dugout before a game, wearing his hard hat and smoking a cigarette. Players would file into the dugout and look out at Comiskey Park, at the wind blowing straight in as it can only in Chicago, and some guy would say, "Nobody's going to hit one out of here tonight.'

"I'd look over at Dick and he'd give me a little wink, and then the game would start and he'd go up there and *whoosh*, he'd hit one in the upper deck.

"I pitched a game in Cleveland where I had the bases loaded and nobody out and I was already down 1–0. There was a double-play ball, short to second to first. Dick had a habit of flipping the ball to the umpire after the third out. He got the ball to complete the double play and flipped it to the umpire, thinking that was the third out, which was rare for Dick because he hardly ever made mistakes on the field. The umpire jumped out of the way, the ball trickled down the right-field line, and the runners from third and second both scored, and we were down 3–0.

"I got the next batter out, and as I was coming off the field, Dick said, 'Sorry about that old timer. I'll get those back for you.'

"He hit two three-run homers, and we won the game 7–3."

The Phillies had signed Allen as a free agent right out of Wampum (Pennsylvania) High School in 1960 for $70,000, a healthy bonus at the time. They sent him first to Elmira, New York, and then to Magic Valley, Idaho, and Williamsport, Pennsylvania. Everything was fine in those first three seasons, but then Allen was assigned to, of all places, Little Rock, Arkansas, where he was the first African American to play for the Arkansas Travelers. He was 21 years old and encountered racism, the likes of which he had not known before.

A punishing power hitter, Dick Allen had a rocky road in Philadelphia.

Townspeople staged parades to protest his presence on their hometown team and scratched racist epithets on his car. Allen answered back by batting .289 with 33 homers and 97 RBIs and leading the league in total bases. It earned him promotion to the Phillies.

Although he had never previously played third base (in the minor leagues he mostly played the outfield and occasionally shortstop and second base), Allen was handed the third-base job in Philadelphia by manager Gene Mauch. The manager tolerated the rookie's inexperience and defensive lapses because of his bat. Allen led the league in runs, triples, extra-base hits, and total bases. He finished in the top five in slugging average, hits, and doubles; hit .318, with 29 homers and 91 RBIs; and was named National League

Rookie of the Year in 1964. That was the year the Phillies suffered arguably the worst collapse in baseball history by blowing a 6½-game lead with 12 games to play. But Allen held up his end by hitting .429 in those 12 games with five doubles, two triples, three home runs, and 11 RBIs.

Allen was born to hit. He knew his ability. He believed in his ability. He believed he could hit anybody and he was no-nonsense at the plate. With a bat in his hands it was as if all his hostility came out, as if he had a grudge against the pitcher and the base-ball. His attitude read, *I'll show you.*

Allen began wearing his batting helmet into the field, leading teammates and opponents to tag him with the nickname "Crash."

Allen's strength and prodigious power seemed to belie the fact it came from a man who stood 5'11" and, in his prime, weighed less than 190 pounds. Swinging a 40-ounce bat, he hit 18 balls that cleared Connie Mack Stadium's 65' left-field grandstand, twice cleared the 65' scoreboard in right center, and hit one ball over the roof in left-center field that traveled an estimated 529 feet, causing Willie Stargell to say, "Now I know why [Phillies fans] boo Richie all the time. When he hits a home run, there's no souvenir."

The booing began in 1965. While some of it was racially motivated, much of the booing was brought on by Allen himself. He got into a fistfight with teammate Frank Thomas. He clashed with other Phillies. He was rude, aloof, and unfriendly to fans and chronically late to the ballpark, often arriving after batting practice and just in time for the start of the game.

When the booing was accompanied by fans showering him with fruit, ice cubes, and batteries, Allen began wearing his batting helmet into the field, leading teammates and opponents to tag him with the nickname "Crash Helmet" and later, simply "Crash."

In 1969, when the Phillies moved Allen to first base, things got so bad that he began to scratch messages in the first-base coach's box with his spikes.

BOO!

GET ME OUT OF HERE!

Allen got his wish after the 1969 season, when he was traded to the Cardinals. Upon arrival in St. Louis, Allen announced that thereafter, he wanted to be called Dick instead of Richie, which he said was "a little boy's name."

By any name, Richie or Dick, he was an enigma, one of the greatest hitters in baseball history and one of its most misunderstood players. He could be charming one moment and contentious the next. He could be fiercely competitive one game and totally uninterested the next. He hit 20 or more home runs 10 times, drove in 90 runs or more six times, batted over .300 seven times, and hit some of the longest shots ever recorded—and yet he kept getting traded. He was sent packing five times in six years, from the Phillies to the Cardinals to the Dodgers to the White Sox to the Braves and finally back to the Phillies.

With the White Sox in 1972, he had his greatest season, a .308 average and a league-leading 37 home runs and 113 RBIs, earning him his only Most Valuable Player Award in a landslide vote over Joe Rudi and Sparky Lyle.

Allen retired in 1977—too young at age 35—after playing in 54 games with the Oakland Athletics. He left baseball with a lifetime batting average of .292, with 351 home runs and 1,119 RBIs in 15 seasons. For a while he was the lead singer for the Ebonistics, a doo-wop group. Later he trained thoroughbred racehorses.

Almost 40 years after he retired, Dick Allen's name is still among the Phillies top ten all-time in home runs, slugging percentage, and intentional walks. He's still waiting for a call from Cooperstown.

Players like **Scott Rolen** are easy to talk about because they are no-nonsense guys. Players like that will give you all they have. They do the little things to win ballgames, like running the bases and being in the right place at the right time on defense. Where instincts are concerned, I put Rolen among those at the top of the list in Phillies history.

Rolen arrived in the big leagues in 1996 and from day one, the Phillies were convinced they had the successor at third base to Mike Schmidt, who had retired a few years earlier. Scott was a lot like Schmidt in that he anticipated the ball coming to him and knew what he wanted to do with it when he got it. He made some brilliant plays, backhanding smashes down the line, rolling on the ground, charging and fielding balls with his bare hand and throwing to first in one motion. He made plays at third base fans hadn't seen in Philly since Schmidt.

Rolen won the Gold Glove in 1998, only his second full season with the Phillies. He won it again in 2000 and in 2001. The Phillies might have had Schmidt's third-base successor for many years had Rolen stayed. He was a guy who kept his feelings inside a lot, the type who resented getting ripped or

Scott Rolen accepts the 1999 Gold Glove Award for his stellar fielding performance.

what he perceived as being lied to. It hurt him and he fumed inside, but he never let it affect his play. He kept going out there, making plays in the field and hitting 31 home runs in 1998, batting .298 in 2000, and driving in 107 runs in 2001. But all the while, Rolen wasn't happy.

When he finally opened his mouth, it was to complain that the Phillies were not trying hard enough to put a winning team on the field. That was in 2002, when the Phillies were in the midst of their eighth losing season within nine years. Rolen demanded a trade and got his wish when the Phillies sent him to the Cardinals.

Ironically, since Rolen left, the Phillies have not had a losing season.

It wasn't all Rolen's fault that he was traded away. The powers that be could have handled him better. Not all players are alike. They don't all respond to threats the same way. Management has to know which buttons to push and which not to push, who to push against and who not to push against. Rolen was one of those guys who didn't respond to getting his buttons pushed. Which is unfortunate, because he should have been one of those players, like Schmidt, who played his entire career with the Phillies.

76

Ironically, since Rolen left, the Phillies have not had a losing season, while winning five NL East titles, two pennants, and one World Series.

Meanwhile, Rolen was traded by the Cardinals to the Blue Jays and then to the Reds, but has continued to play spectacular third base and deliver as a middle-of-the-order hitter and run producer.

Despite a series of debilitating injuries and surgery on his shoulder and finger, Rolen has won eight Gold Gloves (only Brooks Robinson and Schmidt, among third basemen, have won more) and been named to the All-Star team seven times. He has great range and a very accurate arm. I put Rolen right up there with the greatest third basemen I have seen: Brooks Robinson, Ron Santo, Clete Boyer, and Mike Schmidt. Rolen doesn't take a back seat to any of them.

Before Mike Schmidt came along, **Willie "Puddin' Head" Jones** was the standard by which all Phillies third basemen were measured. A dependable clutch hitter and a run producer with some pop in his bat, and he was a magician in the field, leading the National League's third basemen in fielding percentage five times, in putouts seven times, and in assists and double plays twice, posting a career fielding percentage of .963. No less an authority than

Puddin' Head Jones had 13 terrific years in the Phillies uniform. *Courtesy of Getty Images*

Robin Roberts once said he rated Jones second to Brooks Robinson among all of the third basemen he had seen.

Legend has it that Jones' mother gave her son his nickname from a popular 1930s song, "Wooden Head, Puddin' Head Jones."

Puddin' Head arrived in Philadelphia in 1947 and remained there for 13 of his 15 major-league seasons. Had the Gold Glove been awarded prior to 1957, by which time Jones was in his decline, he undoubtedly would have won the award several times.

Despite being underrated and overlooked by baseball historians, Pinky Whitney has earned his place in Phillies history.

From 1949 to 1953 he never drove in fewer than 70 runs or hit fewer than 18 homers. In 1949 he tied a major-league record on April 20 when he hit four consecutive doubles against the Boston Braves. He made the All-Star team in 1950 and '51 and was a mainstay for the 1950 NL-champion Whiz Kids, batting .267 with 25 homers, 88 RBIs, and 100 runs scored. He batted a respectable .286 in the World Series.

When he retired, Jones had accumulated 190 home runs and 812 RBIs, and all but 10 of the homers and 59 of the RBIs came with the Phillies, for whom he hit six career grand slams, at the time second in team history to Mike Schmidt.

He had a lifetime batting average of .295, with 93 home runs and 927 RBIs in 12 major-league seasons. Four seasons he batted over .300. Four seasons he drove in more than 100 runs. Twice he had 200 hits.

He had a fielding percentage of .961 in his 1,358 games at third base and led National League third basemen in fielding three times. (Gold Gloves were not awarded in his day.) He was the starting third baseman for the National League in the fourth All-Star Game in 1936 and drove in the second run with a sacrifice fly in the second inning against Lefty Grove in the NL's 4–3 victory.

Despite all of his superlatives, hardly anybody remembers him—not even the most rabid of baseball fans.

He is **Arthur Carter (Pinky) Whitney** of San Antonio, Texas, and his relative anonymity may be because of these factors:

- In 10 seasons with the Phillies the team finished eighth five times, seventh twice, and had a winning record just once.

- He was overshadowed by his own teammates Cy Williams, Chuck Klein, and Dolph Camilli.
- He suffered by comparison to more famous National League third basemen Pie Traynor, Pepper Martin, and Arky Vaughan.

Despite being underrated and overlooked by baseball historians, Pinky Whitney has earned his place among the five best third basemen in Phillies history.

The Phillies acquired Whitney in the minor league draft and he broke in with an excellent rookie season in 1928, batting .301 with 103 RBIs. He followed that up the next season with a .327 average and 200 hits, one of four Phillies with 200 hits. (The 1929 Phillies are the only team in National League history to have four batters with 200 hits. The others were Chuck Klein, Lefty O'Doul, and Fresco Thompson. Still, the Phillies had a losing record and finished fifth, further evidence that it's all about the pitching.)

Whitney drove in more than 100 runs in four of his first five seasons in Philadelphia, but when his batting average and run production began to slip, he was traded to the Boston Braves during the 1933 season. Three years later, he returned to the Phillies and batted .341 in 1937, his final season as a regular.

Statistical Summaries

All statistics are for player's Phillies career only.

HITTING

G = Games

H = Hits

HR = Home runs

RBI = Runs batted in

SB = Stolen bases

BA = Batting average

Third Baseman	Years	G	H	HR	RBI	SB	BA
Mike Schmidt *Belted game-winning two-run homer off Rollie Fingers in eighth inning of 1981 All-Star Game*	1972–89	2,404	2,234	548	1,595	174	.267
Dick Allen *Drew five walks (three intentional) vs. Giants on 8/16/68*	1963–69, 1975–76	1,070	1,143	204	655	86	.290
Scott Rolen *Hit his first two career homers at Dodger Stadium on 8/21/96*	1996–2002	844	880	150	559	71	.282

continued	Years	G	H	HR	RBI	SB	BA
Willie Jones *Led NL third basemen in putouts and assists in both 1949 and 1950*	1947–59	1,520	1,400	180	753	39	.258
Pinky Whitney *Drove in a run in 10 consecutive games (11 RBIs) from 6/19/31 to 6/27/31*	1928–33, 1936–39	1,157	1,329	69	734	34	.307

FIELDING

PO = Putouts

A = Assists

E = Errors

DP = Double plays

TC/G = Total chances divided by games played

FA = Fielding average

Third Baseman	PO	A	E	DP	TC/G	FA
Mike Schmidt	1,591	5,045	313	450	3.1	.955
Dick Allen	466	1,074	117	101	3.0	.929
Scott Rolen	693	1,667	86	142	2.9	.965
Willie Jones	1,907	2,760	79	257	3.2	.963
Pinky Whitney	1,175	2,064	134	183	3.1	.960

SIX

Left Fielder

It's been more than 100 years since **Ed Delahanty** played for the Phillies, and I still am unable to find anyone to replace him as the greatest left fielder in Phillies history—and believe me, I've tried.

They called him "Big Ed" because at 6'1" and ranging from 175 to 190 pounds, in his time (at the turn of the 20th century) he was considered a giant of a man.

As a baseball player, Big Ed was the Ty Cobb, Babe Ruth, Ted Williams, Henry Aaron, Pete Rose, and Rickey Henderson of his day all rolled in one. He was a five-tool player long before the term was in vogue and the centerpiece of baseball's foremost dynasty, the oldest and best of five brothers who played Major League Baseball.

Delahanty lived a glamorous and envied life as a national sports idol but met a tragic and premature end at the age of 35.

This is a view of Delahanty the batter from a rival pitcher: "When you pitch to Delahanty, you just want to shut your eyes, say a prayer, and chuck the ball. The Lord only knows what'll happen after that."

1. ED DELAHANTY

2. DEL ENNIS

3. GREG LUZINSKI

4. PAT BURRELL

5. SHERRY MAGEE

This is a view of Delahanty the man: "Men who met Ed Delahanty had to admit he was a handsome fellow, although there was an air about him that indicated he was a roughneck at heart and no man to tamper with. He had that wide-eyed, half-smiling, ready-for-anything look that is characteristic of a certain type of Irishman. He had a towering impatience, too, and a taste for liquor and excitement. He created plenty of excitement for opponents and spectators when he laid his tremendous bat against a pitch."

Born in Cleveland, Delahanty broke into professional baseball at age 19 in 1887 with Mansfield in the Ohio State League. A year later, his contract was sold to Philadelphia (they were the Quakers at the time) for $1,500. He joined the team primarily as a second baseman and struggled with a .228 average and 47 errors in 74 games. The next year, he raised his average 65 points and jumped to Cleveland in the newly formed Players League. The league folded after only one year, so back Delahanty went to Philadelphia (they were the Phillies by then), where he put his second-base days behind him. He moved to the outfield and became a star, the premier slugger of the 1890s in the opinion of many.

I realize Delahanty played in an era when there were no such things as closers, split-finger fastballs, cut fastballs, and night baseball; gloves were small, flat pieces of leather without the large webbings common in today's game; and defense was mediocre at best. Nevertheless, you can't overlook some of the numbers Delahanty put up. For instance:

- He led the National League in batting with a .410 average in 1899.
- He led the league in RBIs in 1893 with 146, in 1896 with 126, and in 1899 with 137.
- He led the league in home runs in 1893 with 19 and in 1896 with 13.
- He led the league in stolen bases in 1898 with 58.
- Three times he batted over .400 and finished his career with a .346 average, the fifth-highest in history.
- In a four-year span from 1893 to 1896, he drove in 511 runs, an average of 128 per year.
- He's the only player in baseball history to hit both four home runs in a game (July 13, 1896) and four doubles in a game (May 13, 1899).

In the outfield, he was said to have a strong arm that accounted for 238 career outfield assists, great speed that gave him exceptional range, and nonstop hustle.

Big Ed Delahanty was one of five baseball-playing brothers in Major League Baseball at the turn of the 20ᵗʰ century. *Courtesy of Getty Images*

In addition to his on-field success, Delahanty may also be considered as the first baseball agent, unofficial though it was.

As the 1901 season ended, Big Ed was growing increasingly frustrated. He had batted .354 that season with 192 hits, a league-leading 38 doubles, 16 triples, eight home runs, 108 RBIs, and 29 stolen bases. Despite those dominant statistics, he was still earning just $3,000, slightly higher he was paid more than a decade earlier. Nearing his 34ᵗʰ birthday, he was uneasy over his future in baseball.

The American League had been formed with owners who had deep pockets and were ready, willing, and able to compete with the established National League for talent—a fact that did not escape notice of the sly Ed Delahanty. It is not surprising, then, that Delahanty and eight of his Phillies teammates would make up the bulk of the American League's Washington Senators in 1902. There is no evidence that Delahanty received a percentage from his teammates, but reports that his Washington contract called for a $4,000 salary plus a $1,000 signing bonus were an indication that Delahanty had been the conduit between the Senators and the former Phillies players.

Delahanty gave the Senators and the fledgling league credibility. He batted .376 with 43 doubles, 14 triples, 10 home runs, and 93 RBIs for the Senators in 1902, but by the end of the season, his life was spinning out of control. His wife became ill and Delahanty, who always liked the bottle, began binge drinking and gambling heavily. Seriously in debt, he tried to jump out of his Senators contract by holding out.

Del Ennis must be the most underappreciated, underrated, and overlooked Phillie.

On July 2, 1903, Delahanty, drinking heavily, was on a train headed from Detroit to New York. Drunk and disorderly, he was ordered off the train by the conductor soon after it had crossed the International Railway Bridge into Buffalo. Delahanty left the train and walked onto the bridge and either jumped or fell to his death into the Niagara River. He was three months away from his 36th birthday.

If **Del Ennis** isn't the most underappreciated, underrated, and overlooked player in baseball history, he certainly must be the most underappreciated, underrated, and overlooked Phillie.

He played 14 major-league seasons, 11 of them with the Phillies (1946–56). He was a three-time National League All-Star—twice as starter—led the league in 1950 with 126 RBIs, drove in 100 or more runs seven times, and hit 20 or more home runs nine times. He's on the Phillies' all-time top 10 list in games played, at-bats, runs, hits, singles, doubles, triples, home runs, extra-base hits, RBIs, and total bases.

Ennis hit 288 career home runs—more than Roger Maris, Larry Doby, Joe Torre, Steve Garvey, Don Mattingly, and Hall of Famers Hack Wilson, Roy Campanella, Ryne Sandberg, Joe Morgan, Brooks Robinson, and Robin Yount.

He drove in 1,284 runs—more than Hank Greenberg, Gil Hodges, Pie Traynor, Bobby Doerr, Zack Wheat, Gary Carter, Bill Dickey, Chuck Klein, Earl Averill, Tony Gwynn, Dick Allen, and Kirby Puckett.

He had a lifetime batting average of .284—higher than Willie Stargell, Andre Dawson, Tony Perez, Ralph Kiner, Cal Ripken Jr., Ernie Banks, Eddie Mathews, Willie McCovey, and Carlton Fisk.

And yet in his years of eligibility for the Hall of Fame, he managed to receive only five votes (three in 1966 and two in 1967).

Del Ennis connects against the Cincinnati Reds in a 1950 game.

Ennis was a local boy, born and raised in Philadelphia and signed by the Phillies in 1943 at age 18 out of Olney High School, where he was an All-State fullback and a baseball star. The Phillies sent him to Trenton in the Class B Interstate League, where he batted .348 with 18 homers and 16 triples. The Phillies were set to promote the teenager to the big club in a September call-up, but Ennis was inducted into the U.S. Navy instead. He spent most of the next two years in the Pacific Islands and rose to the rank of petty officer third class.

Ennis obtained his discharge from the navy on April 5, 1946, 11 days before the start of the baseball season. A week later, he reported to the Phillies without the benefit of spring training. He made his major-league debut on April 28 as a pinch-hitter for pitcher Ken Raffensberger in the seventh inning of the first game of a doubleheader against the Boston Braves in Fenway Park. He grounded out to shortstop.

For the next 10 years, Ennis became a fixture in left field and one of the most feared hitters in the National League.

Two days later, the 21-year-old started in left field, batted third, and got his first major-league hit against the Pirates in Forbes Field. He would go on to play in 141 games, bat .313 with 17 homers and 73 runs batted in, and finish eighth in the National League's MVP voting. He was the first recipient of the *Sporting News'* rookie award (the official Rookie of the Year award would be presented for the first time the following year).

For the next 10 years, Ennis became a fixture in left field and in the middle of the Phillies' batting order and one of the most feared hitters in the National League. He was the Phillies' chief power source in 1950 when they won their first National League pennant in 35 years, batting .311, hitting 31 homers, and driving in a league-leading 126 RBIs to finish fourth in the NL Most Valuable Player voting behind teammate Jim Konstanty, Stan Musial, and Eddie Stanky and ahead of teammates Granny Hamner and Robin Roberts.

In the nine-year period from 1949 to 1957, Ennis had more RBIs than every player except Stan Musial. In Ennis' 14-year career he was in the top 10 in batting average three times, home runs eight times, RBIs 10 times, total bases six times, and MVP voting eight times.

When I joined the Phillies after they acquired me from Atlanta for pitcher Bob Walk in a trade just before the start of the 1981 season, I was taking the position that had been held by one of the most popular players the Phillies ever had.

If the fans were expecting me to be another **Greg Luzinski**, a guy who could hit 30 home runs (he had hit 30 or more for the Phillies three times with a high of 39 just four years before), they were going to be disappointed. I had never hit 30 home runs in my career. In fact, I had hit 20 or more only

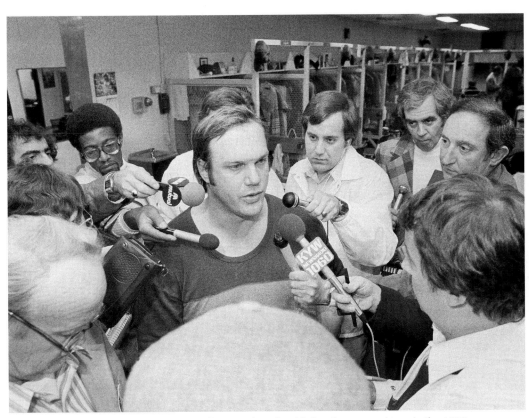

Greg Luzinski is the center of media attention after hitting the game-winner in the 1980 NLCS.

twice. I was a different type of player than Luzinski, but then I was being asked to replace the Philadelphia icon.

I soon found out firsthand what a favorite Luzinski was. I also had the opportunity to fully appreciate the Phillies fans, their knowledge of the game, their passion, and their loyalty. As a player, you never have any doubt where you stand with those fans. They'll let you know loud and clear if they approve or disapprove of your performance. Early on in my stay, they disapproved.

The year before I arrived there, the Phillies, with Luzinski in left field, had won the first World Series in their history. Then the Phillies had traded for me, a left fielder. To make matters worse, five days after I was traded to the Phillies they sold Luzinski to the White Sox. It was apparent what was going on, and the Philly fans didn't like it one bit. I can't say I blamed them.

$\mathcal{B}$ecause of his fierce competitiveness, his work ethic, his loyalty, his leadership, his affability and his willingness to subjugate his personal résumé for the good of the team, Gary "Sarge" Matthews has managed to find gainful employment in several areas of Major League Baseball after his playing days.

In the more than two decades since the end of his distinguished 16-year major-league career with the San Francisco Giants, Atlanta Braves, Philadelphia Phillies, Chicago Cubs, and Seattle Mariners—during which he was the National League Rookie of the Year in 1973 and Most Valuable Player of the National League Championship Series 10 years later, Sarge has been a minor- and major-league hitting instructor and first base coach with the Cubs, a major-league hitting coach for the Toronto Blue Jays and Milwaukee Brewers, broadcaster for the Blue Jays, and is currently a television analyst with the Phillies.

He is widely known and admired throughout baseball by both teammates and opponents and is especially beloved by his legion of former colleagues, several of whom were not only willing but eager to profess their admiration and affection for a (first-class) Sarge.

Garry Maddox grew up in San Pedro, California, about 40 miles south of Gary Matthews' hometown of San Fernando. They played high school baseball at the same time, were drafted by the Giants in the same year, and were scouted and signed by the same man, George Genovese. Yet they never heard of one another in high school and wouldn't meet for another few years.

Maddox had played 63 games in 1968 in the Giants' minor-league system with Salt Lake City and Fresno and then was drafted by the army, spending the next two years fulfilling his military obligation. Matthews, meanwhile, missed the 1968 season—and the draft—because of knee surgery. Upon Maddox's discharge from the army, he was invited to join the Giants' Instructional League team in Arizona and was assigned to room with Matthews, who had just completed his second minor-league season. The two young outfield prospects would become the closest of friends as well as teammates.

Although he's only some 10 months older than Maddox, Matthews was looked upon by Maddox as something of a role model and mentor.

—Phil Pepe

GARRY MADDOX: I had just returned from Vietnam, and Gary kind of took me under his wing. He let me borrow his car and wear his clothes. We became close friends and still are to this day. I consider him my best friend.

As young players with the Giants [Maddox made his major-league debut in April 1972, Matthews five months later], Willie Mays was the big influence on both of our careers. Early on, we learned to play the game from guys like Mays and Willie McCovey. Mays, being who he was, when he said something, you listened. He only had to tell you something, and you would do it. Gary and I both used the MacGregor Kangaroo gloves that we got from Willie. Every spring, the MacGregor representative showed up in camp with a supply of gloves for Mays. Gary and I were like two young sparrows flying around and chirping, waiting for Willie to feed us with new gloves.

[On May 4, 1975, the Giants traded Maddox to the Phillies. He would remain with the Phillies for the rest of his career, retiring after playing in only six games in the 1986 season. In 1981 the Phillies acquired Gary Matthews in a trade with the Atlanta Braves and the two friends would be reunited as Phillies teammates for three seasons.]

In 1983 we had some veteran players who were unhappy with their playing time and didn't try to hide it. Gary was one of those players, but what impressed me was that when guys were sitting around and complaining, Gary went out and worked even harder. He never complained. He had a great attitude and he showed it in practice and in games by going as hard as he could. I observed that and it helped me change my attitude, and how I looked at things. He taught me that just because you may be having your own issues, you don't let your teammates down. And to top it off, that was the year we won the pennant and Gary was the MVP of the championship series.

That was also the year Pete Rose pinned the name "Sarge" on Gary. And Gary is such a free spirit, he embraced the name and he milked it. When he went to Chicago and played with the Cubs, he started saluting when he took the field.

Gary led through example. He led by talking to you when things were not going your way. Nobody went base to base to break up double plays any harder than Gary. When we were teammates, we had this thing going on. If we went on a postgame radio or TV show and there was an honorarium—cash or a gift certificate, whatever it was—we would split it 50/50. Also, if a pitcher threw at either one of us, the other one would try to hit the ball back through the middle as a way of sending a message to the pitcher.

Gary and Pete Rose were two of my all-time teammates. They fit so well together because they were so much alike. Nobody outworked them. They both had unselfish attitudes. Those are the kinds of players you want on your team. The way it has carried on for Sarge is that he has always found some place to go. Somebody has always wanted him. Most guys have trouble transitioning and finding jobs in baseball, but Gary always has one because people like him so much and think so highly of him. He's a great person with a great work ethic, and to me, he's a tremendous friend. There's nothing I wouldn't do for him.

[Matthews was in the twilight of his career in 1984 when the Phillies traded him to the Cubs. There he would find a kindred spirit in former Cub Ron Santo, then a broadcaster with the team.]

RON SANTO: Sarge is a guy I would take with me in my foxhole. His nickname tells it all about him. He was a leader. Think of a marine drill sergeant—tough, demanding (on himself and others), competitive, aggressive.

Sarge speaks his mind. He's a guy who knows what he's talking about. He played the game the way it should be played. He didn't just walk out there and swing the bat and field the ball; he knew how to play the game and he understands the game as well as anybody.

I've always admired him for the way he played. He was daring and mean on the bases, taking the extra base, sliding hard into second to break up double plays, and he understood hitting. Who wouldn't want a guy like that on his team?

When the Cubs got him, his best days were behind him, but he had enough left to make an impact and to make an impression on his younger teammates. His veteran leadership helped the Cubs win a division title in 1984.

[When Dusty Baker became manager of the Chicago Cubs in 2003, he had known Gary Matthews only as an opponent, never as a teammate, yet he chose Sarge to be his hitting coach.]

DUSTY BAKER: I played against Sarge a lot, and even though we were opponents, we got to be good friends and I always admired his approach to hitting and his enthusiasm for the game. He brought a lot to the table. For two years, he did an excellent job as my hitting coach.

As a result, I got booed a lot in the first week or so. It took me a while to win over the fans, and I like to think I did just that. I wound up hitting .301 that season. (Luzinski, who had batted over .300 three times in the 1970s and averaged .281 in his 11 seasons with the Phillies, had slipped to .228 in 1980.)

Greg was a blue-collar player who looked and played like his nickname, "the Bull." He stood 6'1", weighed upwards of 220 with massive arms and a thick neck, and was a masher whose game was all power, not speed and grace. When Luzinski batted .300 you knew it was well-earned because Greg had no foot speed. There were no infield hits for him.

In the 1970s the Phillies were looking for a legitimate power hitter, and Luzinski fit that mold very well. When Mike Schmidt came along, he was paired with Luzinski, and the two of them averaged almost 66 home runs a year, a big help in getting the Phillies four NL East titles.

Greg led the National League in RBIs in 1975 with 120, but his best year came two years later when he finished third in home runs with 39, second in RBIs with 130, ninth in batting with a .309 average, second in slugging percentage with .594, and came in second to George Foster of the Reds in the MVP voting. What is mindboggling to me is that Luzinski had 171 hits and struck out 140 times in 554 at-bats—so when he made contact, he batted .413.

Luzinski's popularity endures in Philadelphia. He lives in Florida but is a frequent visitor to Citizens Bank Park, where he opened Bull's Barbecue restaurant. Greg is in the Wall of Fame and he's among the Phillies' all-time top 10 in home runs, RBIs, walks, and sacrifice flies.

For reasons I can't fathom, **Pat "the Bat" Burrell** never caught on with those discriminating fans of Philadelphia despite having nine productive seasons with the Phillies. In that time he hit 251 home runs, drove in 827 runs, and helped the Phillies win the World Series in 2008. (He also helped the Giants beat the Phillies in the NLCS two years later.)

In high school, Burrell was a two-sport star, a third baseman and a quarterback who competed against future New England Patriot Tom Brady. Burrell gave up football, attended the University of Miami to play baseball, and was selected by the Phillies as the first overall pick in the 1998 amateur draft.

Pat "the Bat" Burrell had a productive nine-year stint in Philadelphia.

As a Phillie, Burrell hit more home runs than Chuck Klein, Greg Luzinski, Dick Allen, and Bobby Abreu, and drove in more runs than Luzinski and Abreu. But he also struck out 1,273 times, an average of 141 per year, more strikeouts than any Phillie except Mike Schmidt.

When Burrell filed for free agency in 2009, the Phillies turned the page and let him walk.

Sherwood "Sherry" Magee is the baseball star nobody knows, the almost–Hall of Famer who just missed making it to Cooperstown, a Phillies outfielder in the dead-ball era who performed ahead of the curve.

In 16 major-league seasons, 11 of them with the Phillies, Magee had a batting average of .291, hit 83 home runs, drove in 1,176 runs, had 2,169 hits, and had 441 stolen bases (a remarkable 23 of them of home plate). He was in the National League's top 10 in home runs and RBIs seven times in the 10-

year span from 1905 to 1914 and was said to be one of the best defensive out-fielders of his day.

If those aren't Hall of Fame numbers, Magee certainly had Hall of Fame seasons. In 1907 he led the league with 85 RBIs, and his .328 average was second to Honus Wagner's .350. In 1910 Magee led the league in batting, RBIs, runs, total bases, on-base percentage, and slugging average; he was second in doubles and triples. In 1914 he was first in hits, doubles, RBIs, extra bases, total bases, and slugging in a league that had such stars as Honus Wagner, Jake Daubert, Zack Wheat, Max Carey, Rabbit Maranville, Gavvy Cravath, Fred Luderus, and Casey Stengel.

Sherry Magee, a standout in the dead-ball era, hasn't gotten his due recognition. *Courtesy of Getty Images*

In one game against the Cardinals, Magee stole second, third, and home in the ninth inning. In another game against the Cubs, he stole home twice.

Reading about him convinced me that Sherry Magee was a player I would have liked. He was aggressive and daring and openly critical when he believed his teammates weren't trying their best or were playing the game improperly. He also had a temper. Once after being ejected for arguing a third strike, Magee got into a beef with umpire Bill Finneran and decked him with one punch.

Magee played his final season with Cincinnati in 1919 and was an innocent and unsuspecting part of baseball infamy: the so-called Black Sox scandal.

When the Phillies finished a disappointing sixth in 1914 and fired their manager, Magee campaigned for the job. When they chose someone else as manager, he asked to be traded. The Phillies accommodated him and dealt him to the Boston Braves. With Magee, the Braves finished in second place in 1915; however, the Phillies won their first pennant.

Magee played his final season with Cincinnati in 1919 and was an innocent and unsuspecting part of baseball infamy: the so-called Black Sox scandal in which eight members of the Chicago White Sox conspired to throw the World Series to Magee's Reds. Magee was neither dumper nor dumpee. Due to illness, he was reduced to pinch-hitting and appeared twice—in two of the three games the White Sox played on the level, both times beating the Reds.

The Reds did not bring Magee back in 1920, so he went back down to the minor leagues and played for seven more years before jumping to the other side and becoming an umpire. After umpiring in the minor leagues for a couple of years, Magee reached the National League in 1928, but the following spring he contracted pneumonia and died at the age of 44.

Statistical Summaries

All statistics are for player's Phillies career only.

HITTING

G = Games
H = Hits
HR = Home runs
RBI = Runs batted in
SB = Stolen bases
BA = Batting average

Left Fielder	Years	G	H	HR	RBI	SB	BA
Ed Delahanty *Had 11 games with five or more hits, second only to Ty Cobb (15)*	1888–89, 1891–1901	1,557	2,597	101	1,466	455	.346
Del Ennis *Only career three-homer game vs. Cardinals, 7/23/55*	1946–56	1,630	1,812	259	1,124	44	.286
Greg Luzinski *Drew league-leading 17 intentional walks in 1975*	1970–80	1,289	1,299	223	811	29	.281

continued	Years	G	H	HR	RBI	SB	BA
Pat Burrell *42 career homers vs. Mets (through 2011) is 16 more than next-highest team (Marlins)*	2000–08	1,306	1,166	251	827	5	.257
Sherry Magee *Stole four bases in a game twice in 1906 (7/12, 8/3)*	1904–14	1,521	1,647	75	886	387	.299

FIELDING

PO = Putouts

A = Assists

E = Errors

DP = Double plays

TC/G = Total chances divided by games played

FA = Fielding average

Left Fielder	PO	A	E	DP	TC/G	FA
Ed Delahanty	2,613	216	153	42	2,5	.949
Del Ennis	3,286	134	105	25	2.2	.970
Greg Luzinski	1,845	67	55	8	1.6	.972
Pat Burrell	1,842	86	47	10	1.7	.976
Sherry Magee	2,829	136	100	31	2.2	.967

SEVEN

Center Fielder

Saying that **Richie Ashburn** was popular in Philadelphia would be inadequate and a gross understatement. *Beloved* is a better word—beloved as a player *and* a broadcaster. He was a Philadelphia icon for half a century, endeared in the hearts of the Phillies and their fans.

Ashburn came out of Tilden, Nebraska, and signed with the Phillies as an 18-year-old free agent in 1945. Three years later he began a sensational and unbroken 12-year run as the Phillies' center fielder and leadoff hitter in a career that would lead to election to the National Baseball Hall of Fame by hitting .333, leading the league with 32 stolen bases, making the All-Star team, and finishing third in the National League Rookie of the Year voting.

1. Richie Ashburn

2. Cy Williams

3. Billy Hamilton

4. Garry Maddox

5. Tony Gonzalez

While playing for a Phillies team that finished in the second division six times, finished last twice, and had only four winning seasons in 12 years, Ashburn nonetheless put up some exceptional numbers. He batted above .300 eight times, won two batting titles and was runner-up twice, led the National League in walks four times, in hits three times, and in triples twice. He scored fewer than 84 runs in a season only once and made the All-Star team four times.

Standout player and beloved announcer, Richie Ashburn is one of Philadelphia's most respected figures.

What I heard about Ashburn when I talked to his teammate Robin Roberts was that he was a tough out. Richie—who was called "Whitey" by teammates, friends, and fans—was durable (in 10 of his 12 seasons with the Phillies, he played in at least 151 games and from 1949 to 1960 he played in 1,828 of his team's 1,855 games, good for .985 percent) and he was a singles machine. A whopping 82 percent of his 2,574 hits were singles. On May 20, 1951, in a doubleheader against the Pirates, Ashburn rapped out eight singles in 11 at-bats.

While his penchant for hitting singles made him the ideal leadoff man, it no doubt kept him out of his rightful place in the Hall of Fame for years. In his 15 years of eligibility, he failed to garner more than the 41.7 percent of the vote he received from members of the Baseball Writers Association of America in 1978. He was finally elected by the Veterans Committee in 1995.

*H*is warmth, his charm, his innocence, his naivete, his malaprops, his humor, and his self-deprecation all combined to make Richie Ashburn as much of a Philadelphia icon in the broadcast booth as he was on the baseball diamond.

He began his broadcast career in 1963, partnered with Byrum Saam, a Philly legend and Hall of Fame broadcaster. Later, he teamed with another Hall of Fame broadcaster and Philadelphia legend, Harry Kalas. Ashburn and Kalas became close friends. On the air, Kalas brought out the best in Ashburn, referring to him as "His Whiteness" and serving as straight man to Ashburn's wry humor.

During one game, Ashburn was discussing the many superstitions that consumed him as a ballplayer. One such superstition was taking the bat he used after a good day at the plate to bed with him to make certain he had that same bat for the next game.

"In my day as a player," Ashburn said, "I slept with a lot of old bats."

Ashburn's down-home style included sending birthday wishes to friends, fans, and regular listeners. He also, on occasion, would wonder aloud if the staff of a nearby establishment, Celebre's Pizzeria, was tuned to the game. Twenty minutes later, several pizzas would magically arrive in the radio booth. Ashburn continued the practice until he was told to cease and desist because Celebre's Pizzeria was not a sponsor of Phillies broadcasts and any mention would therefore be considered free advertising and against FCC regulations.

Ashburn was informed, however, that he could continue announcing birthday wishes.

Undaunted, one night while making birthday announcements, Ashburn said, "I'd like to send out a special birthday wish to the Celebre's twins, Plain and Pepperoni."

Cy Williams was a devastating hitter whose numbers rivaled his contemporary, the Great Bambino himself.

his dead-pull, left-handed power was perfect for Philadelphia's Baker Bowl with its cozy right-field wall, only 272 feet from home down the line.

In the decade of the 1920s, Williams was the scourge of the National League with 202 home runs—such a scourge, in fact, that rival managers devised a "Williams Shift" to defend his penchant for pulling the ball to the right side.

After his 41 homers in 1923, Williams shared one more National League home-run title when he hit 30 in 1927 and tied with Chicago's Hack Wilson for the league lead. Williams hit 251 career home runs, 217 of them for the Phillies (he still ranks seventh on their all-time list.) He hit 12 inside-the-park homers, seven grand slams, and, when he no longer was an everyday player he became a potent pinch-hitter, playing until the age of 42 and hitting 11 pinch-hit homers, a major-league record that stood until 1960.

While Williams is best known for his home-run bat, he was a lifetime .292 hitter who batted over .300 six times, including a personal high of .345 in 1926.

Despite his excellent credentials, Williams never came close to being elected to the Hall of Fame. During his years of eligibility, the most votes he received was 11, or 5.7 percent of the vote from the Baseball Writers Association.

When he retired from baseball, Williams took advantage of his college degree and became a successful architect in Wisconsin.

They called him "Sliding Billy," and for good reason. On a baseball diamond, **Billy Hamilton** spent more time on his belly than a garden-variety snake. He was a trailblazer, an innovator, and the game's first great leadoff hitter.

Hamilton is recognized as the first player to slide headfirst, the first to daringly advance from first base to third on a single, and the first to incorporate the drag bunt as a vital part of his offense.

Although he played for the Phillies only for six seasons—and that was more than a century ago—he still holds several career and season records for the Phillies, including:

- Highest career batting average, .360
- Highest career on-base percentage, .468
- Most career stolen bases, 510
- Most runs scored in a season, 198
- Most stolen bases in a season, 111

In fairness, it must be pointed out that while Hamilton was a Phillie, and until 1898, if a player took one base more than he was otherwise entitled to on a hit or an out, he was credited with a stolen base. However, while it calls into question the exact number of Hamilton's stolen bases, it doesn't diminish his prowess as a base stealer.

In 1937 Hamilton wrote a blistering letter to the editors of the *Sporting News* in which he blasted the paper for questioning his stolen-base records.

"I was and will be the greatest base stealer of all time," he wrote. "I stole over 100 bases on many years and if they ever re-count the record, I will get my just reward."

Indeed, Hamilton stole more than 100 bases in a season four times and official records credit him with 111 steals in 1889 and 1891 and have him third on the all-time list (behind Rickey Henderson and Lou Brock) with 914 career stolen bases. Despite that, he didn't get his just reward of election to the National Baseball Hall of Fame until 1961, 21 years after his death.

Among his distinctions, Hamilton is one of five batters to hit both a leadoff home run and a walkoff home run in the same game, one of three

106

"Sliding Billy" Hamilton was a punishing base runner for the Phillies in the 1890s. He was dealt to the Boston Beaneaters in 1896. *Courtesy of Getty Images*

players to average more than one run for every game played, and one of just two players to steal seven bases in one game.

Hamilton, a diminutive left-handed hitter, 5'6" and 165 pounds, born and raised in Newark, New Jersey, broke into the major leagues in 1888 with the Kansas City Cowboys of the American Association. Two years later, when the struggling Kansas City franchise was forced to disband, Hamilton was sold to the Phillies. Already in place in the Phillies outfield was Sam Thompson. Big Ed Delahanty arrived the following year to form what many believe was the greatest hitting outfield in baseball history.

I go back with Garry Maddox just about longer than anybody in baseball.

In 1894 all three Phillies outfielders batted higher than .400 (Thompson .415, Delahanty .404, and Hamilton .403) and combined for 460 runs, 612 hits, 370 RBIs, and 148 stolen bases in a 128-game season. As a team, the 1894 Phillies batted .350 and scored 1,179 runs, or 9.2 runs per game, but still finished in fourth place in the National League with a record of 71–57, proving that in any era, on any level, you don't win without pitching.

107

For No. 4 on my list of the best center fielders in Phillies history, allow me to get personal. I go back with **Garry Maddox** just about longer than anybody in baseball. We were rookies together with the San Francisco Giants in 1972, teammates and as close as brothers for four seasons with the Giants. We were two Gary M's (even though he one-ups me by having two *R*s in Garry to my one) and we were often confused for one another. We're about the same age and about the same height. I was about 10 or 15 pounds heavier than Garry (I still am) and was known as "the heavier one." When I was traded to the Phillies, Maddox was already there and we were reunited as teammates for three more years.

In 1972 Garry and I were together in the big-league spring-training camp, both of us being touted as part of the Giants' future. We both had extremely good springs, and as camp was about to break we were called in to meet with manager Charlie Fox, his coaches, and a couple of front-office guys.

"What do you want to do?" Fox said. "Do you want to stay up here and sit on the bench, or do you want to go down to Triple A and play?"

Foolish me, I said, "I'd rather go down and play." Garry said he'd rather stay in the big leagues and sit.

Garry Maddox is a great friend and was a great ballplayer. Here he is with Pete Rose in 1981.

Actually, they already had their minds made up about us. We were both sent to Phoenix in the Pacific Coast League. So Garry didn't get his wish—at least not right away. But it didn't take long. He played only 11 games in Phoenix and tore it up, hitting .438 with nine home runs and 22 RBIs before the Giants brought him up to the big club. A few days after he got there the Giants traded Willie Mays to the New York Mets, and Maddox took over in center field, replacing the incomparable and irreplaceable.

Phillies broadcaster Harry Kalas had dubbed Maddox "the Secretary of Defense."

I had a good year in Phoenix. I batted .313, hit 21 homers, and drove in 108 runs (I got a lot of attention because I broke the team record for RBIs held by Dusty Rhodes, the hitting star of the 1954 World Series) and got my ticket to the big leagues punched with a September call-up. I made my major-league debut on September 6, playing right field alongside Maddox and batting leadoff in front of Maddox. For the record, I got my first major-league hit in the second inning and scored when Maddox followed me with a home run.

I also was in the room a few years later, in 1975, when they told Maddox he was being traded to the Phillies for Willie Montanez. The word around the team was that Maddox was being traded because he wasn't very good defensively. What a joke! Maddox went to Philadelphia and won eight consecutive Gold Gloves from 1975 to 1982, as many as Barry Bonds, Paul Blair, and Dwight Evans and more than Curt Flood, Kirby Puckett, and Bobby Bonds.

Phillies broadcaster Harry Kalas had dubbed him "the Secretary of Defense," and both Kalas and Hall of Famer and Mets broadcaster Ralph Kiner are credited with the line, "Two-thirds of the earth is covered by water, the other one-third is covered by Garry Maddox."

Despite that, in my mind Maddox doesn't get enough credit for saving runs. When you talk about defense, one of the first players you think of is Ozzie Smith. He made the Hall of Fame for his defense. Ozzie was a terrific player, and he deserves to be in the Hall of Fame. But Garry Maddox was every bit as good defensively at his position as Ozzie was at his.

When it came to what Maddox could do on a ballfield, I suppose I was spoiled. Others would marvel at some of the catches he made. I never did. Why? Because I came up with him through the minor leagues and I knew what he could do. He did it all the time, so I wasn't surprised at anything he did on defense. I expected it of him. With the Giants, Garry played between Bobby Bonds in right field and me in left and he would tell us to take care of the lines, he had the gaps.

Garry was a guy who was always trying to better himself. I have images of him sitting in front of his locker before games often with his nose in a book. Today, he's a prominent and successful businessman based in his adopted home, Philadelphia.

I come to No. 5 on my list of all-time Phillies center fielders torn between **Tony Gonzalez** and Shane Victorino, but because Gonzalez's career is done and Victorino's is still ongoing, I'm giving the nod to Gonzalez, knowing full well that in a few years, Victorino could replace Gonzalez in that spot.

Tony Gonzalez edges Shane Victorino on my all-time Phillies center-fielder list...for now.

Not to be confused with the great All-Pro tight end of the National Football League, this Tony Gonzalez was a Cuban-born center fielder who played 12 seasons with the Reds, Padres, Angels, Braves, and Phillies and had a lifetime batting average of .286. His best years, nine of them, were with the Phillies and his best season was in 1967 as a Phillie when he batted .339, second in baseball to Roberto Clemente.

Curiously, Tony never made the All-Star team, although he probably should have made it a few times. It's curious considering that three times while he was with the Phillies, he got votes for Most Valuable Player.

The hallmark of Gonzalez was his amazing consistency. In his nine seasons with the Phillies he batted at least .286 six times, scored at least 50 runs six times, drove in 40 or more runs seven times, hit 19 or more doubles five times, and had 40 or more walks six times. Defensively, he had excellent range and an average but accurate arm.

Gonzalez made one lasting contribution to baseball. He was hit by pitches so often that in 1964, he was the first major-league player ever to wear a batting helmet with an earflap; it was constructed especially for him. Today, virtually every batter wears a helmet with an earflap.

Statistical Summaries

All statistics are for player's Phillies career only.

HITTING

G = Games

H = Hits

HR = Home runs

RBI = Runs batted in

SB = Stolen bases

BA = Batting average

Center Fielder	Years	G	H	HR	RBI	SB	BA
Richie Ashburn *Hit 15 of his 29 career home runs at New York's Polo Grounds*	1948–59	1,794	2,217	22	499	199	.311
Cy Williams *Homered in consecutive pinch-hitting appearances, 6/2 and 6/6/28*	1918–30	1,463	1,553	217	795	77	.306
Billy Hamilton *Legged out three triples vs. Reds, 7/14/1891*	1890–95	732	1,084	23	370	510	.360

continued	Years	G	H	HR	RBI	SB	BA
Garry Maddox *Made 12 putouts in 12 innings vs. Pirates, 6/10/84*	1975–86	1,328	1,333	85	566	189	.284
Tony Gonzalez *Didn't commit an error in 276 total chances in 1962*	1960–68	1,118	1,110	77	438	68	.295

FIELDING

PO = Putouts

A = Assists

E = Errors

DP = Double plays

TC/G = Total chances divided by games played

FA = Fielding average

Center Fielder	PO	A	E	DP	TC/G	FA
Richie Ashburn	5,454	154	94	40	3.2	.984
Cy Williams	3,074	173	88	34	2.5	.974
Billy Hamilton	1,721	100	155	33	2.7	.922
Garry Maddox	3,093	64	50	14	2.5	.984
Tony Gonzalez	2,069	63	27	14	2.0	.987

EIGHT

Right Fielder

I seriously doubt any player in major-league history provides a better argument for baseball as a team game than **Charles Herbert "Chuck" Klein,** who was the Phillies' right fielder for 15 seasons in the 1920s, '30s, and '40s.

Here's a guy who was elected to the Hall of Fame, was the first Phillie voted the National League's Most Valuable Player (he was second in the voting two other times), is the only Phillie ever to win the Triple Crown of hitting (batting average, home runs, and RBIs), and is one of only 15 players to hit four home runs in a game. He also led the National League in home runs four times and in RBIs twice, set a Phillies home-run record that lasted for 51 years, and ranks in the team's career top 10 in batting average, hits, doubles, home runs, RBIs, slugging, total bases, extra-base hits, and runs.

1. CHUCK KLEIN

2. SAM THOMPSON AND ELMER FLICK

3. BOBBY ABREU

4. GAVVY CRAVATH

5. JOHNNY CALLISON

In addition, on the Phillies' single-season top 10 list, Klein holds the top three spots in extra-base hits; is first, second, third, and seventh in total bases; second, fourth, and sixth in slugging percentage; first and third in doubles; first, seventh, and 10th in RBIs; second, fourth, sixth, and 10th in hits; and eighth in home runs.

116

Chuck Klein (left) poses with Jimmie Foxx of the Chicago Cubs before game action in 1944, Klein's last season. *Courtesy of Getty Images*

Despite impressive numbers, Klein could not single-handedly lead the Phillies to the Promised Land...or even the first division. In his 15 seasons with the Phillies, Klein played on only one winning team. That was 1932, when the Phillies finished in fourth place with a record of 78–76 and Klein was voted the National League's Most Valuable Player, an award that traditionally goes to a player on a pennant-winning team—or even a second-place team—but rarely to a player on a fourth-place team. The fact is that through no fault of his own, in Klein's 15 years with the Phillies in an eight-team league, the team finished in last place nine times, in seventh place three times, sixth once, fifth once, and fourth once.

Despite impressive numbers, Klein could not single-handedly lead the Phillies to the Promised Land...or even the first division.

Along with his productive bat, Klein was a defensive asset for the Phillies, a right fielder who, in his career, had more assists (194) than errors (135). In 1930 he set a modern (post-1900) major-league record for assists by an outfielder with the staggering total of 44 (the major-league leader in 2011 had 20), and his 194 career assists are one fewer than Willie Mays and more than Richie Ashburn, Barry Bonds, Al Kaline, Dave Winfield, Jesse Barfield, Andre Dawson, and a guy named Matthews—*Senior*, that is.

Purchased by the Phillies from Fort Wayne of the Central League in 1928 for $5,000, Klein was an immediate hit in Philadelphia, batting .360 with 11 homers and 34 RBIs in 64 games. Over the next five seasons, he batted .359 and averaged 138.6 runs, 46.4 doubles, 36 homers, and 138.6 RBIs. Desperate for money, the Phillies sent Klein to the Cubs in 1934 for three players and $65,000. Klein helped the Cubs win the National League pennant in 1935. On May 21, 1936, he was headed back to the Phillies in a two-for-two trade. No money changed hands. Seven weeks later, on July 10, 1936, against the Pirates in Pittsburgh, Klein had his greatest day when he became the first NL player in the modern era to hit four home runs in a game.

Klein's detractors (during his years of eligibility for the Hall of Fame, he never received higher than 27.9 percent of the vote from the Baseball Writers Association of America; he was finally elected by the Veterans Committee in 1980, 22 years after his death) attributed his offensive prowess largely to being a left-handed hitter playing his home games in Philadelphia's Baker Bowl with its cozy right-field fence.

Proving those detractors wrong, while he averaged 16.2 homers in 15 seasons with the Phillies, he averaged 15.3 in three seasons with the Cubs, and while he hit 164 career home runs in Baker Bowl, he hit almost as many (136) in seven other National League parks.

The reality may be that Klein was unappreciated and failed to get the recognition he deserved because he played on such bad teams. Maybe if he had been surrounded by better players he would have been regarded on a par with the sluggers of his day such as Babe Ruth, Lou Gehrig, Jimmie Foxx, Hack Wilson, Mel Ott, and Al Simmons.

I'm going to hedge here, go against the rules and pick **Sam Thompson** and **Elmer Flick** as a tandem for No. 2 on my all-time list of Phillies right fielders mainly because it's difficult to think of one without the other.

Like Jekyll and Hyde, they are so closely linked that it almost seems they were one person using two different names, and there's nobody around today to say they weren't. Both began their careers in the 19th century. Both were

Hall of Famer Sam Thompson was one of the Phillies' first stars. *Courtesy of Getty Images*

Elmer Flick took to the Phils naturally as Thompson's replacement. *Courtesy of Getty Images*

ELMER H. FLICK,
RIGHTFIELDER, PHILAD 1899.

primarily right fielders. Both batted left-handed. And both were elected to the Hall of Fame. In one season, 1898, they were even Phillies teammates.

At the time, Thompson was coming to the end of his brilliant career, 38 years old and suffering with a bad back. To replace him, the Phillies brought up Flick, who took over Thompson's position at right field. As a result, for a 13-year span, 1889–1901, the Phillies' right field was manned by Thompson/Flick.

To dispel any conspiracy theories, there were some obvious differences between Thompson and Flick. Thompson was born in Indiana, Flick in Ohio. At 6'2" and more than 200 pounds, Thompson was a towering figure in his day. Flick was a diminutive 5'9" and 165 pounds.

Thompson began his major-league career in 1885 with the Detroit Wolverines of the National League. In 1887 he batted a league-leading .372, knocked in 166 runs (which stood as the major-league record until Babe

Ruth broke it in 1921), and helped the Wolverines win the pennant and then the World Series against the St. Louis Browns of the American Association.

Two years later, when financial troubles forced the Wolverines to fold and sell off their players, Thompson was purchased by the Philadelphia Quakers for $5,000. Thompson spent 10 seasons with the Phillies, leading the league in home runs twice and in RBIs twice, batting .415 in 1894 (Hugh Duffy of the Boston Beaneaters led the league with .440) and higher than .300 five other times and in 1889, becoming the first major-league player with 20 home runs and 20 stolen bases in the same season.

[Thompson was] the first major-league player with 20 home runs and 20 stolen bases in the same season.

Injuries forced Thompson out and made room for Flick after the 1898 season, but a decade later, Thompson resurfaced to play in eight games with the Detroit Tigers at age 46. He was posthumously elected to the Hall of Fame in 1974.

By 1902 Flick had played four seasons with the Phillies—batting .302, .342, .367, and .333—when he joined several other stars who were seduced by more money to jump to the new American League. To make matters worse for the Phillies and their fans, Flick's jump was just a short hop, to the crosstown Athletics. When the Phillies obtained an injunction prohibiting any player they had under contract from playing for another team in the city, Flick left the Athletics and signed with the Cleveland Naps. To avoid being served with a subpoena, Flick did not accompany the Naps when they played in Philadelphia.

Flick played the remainder of his career, nine years, in Cleveland, where he had his best years. He lived to smell the roses and was elected to the Hall of Fame in 1963. He died eight years later at age 94.

By the middle of his ninth season with the Phillies, **Bobby Abreu** had picked up the reputation of being a "soft" player on defense, meaning he studiously avoided banging into walls or colliding with teammates while chasing fly balls. No matter that in his first eight seasons in Philadelphia Abreu had missed only 41 games and had played in 97 percent of his team's schedule or that he had hit over .300 six times, driven in more than 100 runs four times, hit at least 20 home runs seven times, and stolen at least 19 bases eight times.

The guy is a shade below being a lifetime .300 hitter who seemed at his peak to go 30–30 (30 homers, 30 steals) every year with no problem.

No one knows what Bobby Abreu could have done had he remained in Philadelphia.

Consistency is the name of the game and Bobby was as consistent as anybody who has played for the Phillies, at least in the 40 or so years that I've been around. Still, on July 30, 2006, with Abreu well on his way to his fourth consecutive 100-RBI season (he would eventually get it with another team) and closing in on his 33rd birthday, the Phillies, displeased with Abreu's safety-first approach to defense and believing his career was on the decline, pulled the trigger and traded him to the New York Yankees for four minor-leaguers.

Playing for two teams in the five full seasons since the trade, Abreu has tacked on three more 100-RBI seasons, giving him nine in his career; hit 71 homers; 149 doubles; and stolen 101 bases. He also went past 1,300 RBIs and is bearing down on 300 home runs in his career. He also has won a Gold Glove, a Silver Slugger Award, and was twice named an All-Star.

In short, the native Venezuelan they call "el Comedulce" has had a wonderful career—especially for a player nobody wanted.

Abreu signed as a free agent with the Houston Astros in 1990 as a 16-year-old and spent six seasons in the minor leagues before getting to the big leagues to stay with the Astros in 1997. But after only 74 games over two seasons, the Astros left him unprotected in the 1997 expansion draft. He was selected by the Tampa Bay Devil Rays, but a few hours later they traded him to the Phillies, where he became one of the outstanding hitters in the National League over the next decade...or, until the Phillies, like the Astros and Devil Rays before them, deemed Abreu expendable and shipped him to the Yankees, with whom he continued to put up impressive numbers until leaving to sign as a free agent with the Los Angeles Angels of Anaheim.

Of the four players the Phillies obtained from the Yankees for Abreu, only pitchers Matt Smith and Carlos Monasterios made it to the major leagues. Combined, they appeared in 67 big-league games with a record of 3–6.

In his 16th major-league season, at 37 years of age, Abreu was still going strong. He wasn't the player he once was. He probably wasn't going to hit 30 home runs or drive in 100 runs again, but he was still producing, still playing 140 games or more, still getting double figures in steals.

As his batting-average, home-run, RBI, and stolen-base numbers start their inevitable decline, I hope it doesn't diminish what Abreu has done throughout his magnificent career. I have long believed that the most difficult player to manage is the falling star because he will always feel he's still got it. He'll foul off balls that he should be putting in play, balls that he used to crush, and you think, *Doesn't that guy know he's done?* He thinks he's going to be able to do it. He thinks he's going to come back. That's just the way we're made as human beings. No matter how old we are we say, "I've still got it."

That's why fighters keep coming back, like when Evander Holyfield went back into the ring at age 48. Some of it may be because they need the money, but they wouldn't come back if they didn't think they could kick somebody's butt, if they didn't think they could still hit a 95-mph fastball, if they didn't think they could still throw that pass, like Brett Favre.

An athlete who has been successful never thinks he can't do it any longer. We all go through it. But sooner or later Father Time says your time's up. You can't catch up to a 95-mph fastball any longer. Hey, you're not catching up to it at 88 mph. But you still think, *One more time. I know I can do it.* You can't let it go. The true athlete always thinks he has something left in the tank, and he's usually the last one to realize he has nothing left to give.

Consistency is the name of the game and Bobby was as consistent as anybody who has played for the Phillies.

123

Before Babe Ruth, there was **Gavvy Cravath**, the home-run king of his day, a trailblazer and baseball's premier power hitter in the dead-ball era.

Born Clifford Carlton Cravath in Escondido, California, a suburb of San Diego, Cravath became a star with the Los Angeles Angels of the Pacific Coast League at a time when independent baseball leagues flourished, advancement to the major leagues was uncommon, and many players spent their entire professional careers in the minor leagues.

With the Angels, Cravath earned a reputation as a powerful right-handed hitter. In addition, he also picked up a reputation as a tough-talking, hard-driving player known as a tobacco-chewing, cussing bruiser whose prickly personality earned him the nickname "Cactus."

It was while playing in California that Cravath also acquired his more famous nickname when he hit a ball that struck and killed a seagull in flight and fans began calling him Gavvy, a bastardization of *gaviota*, the Spanish word for *seagull*.

In 1908, after five seasons in the Pacific Coast League, Cravath got his chance when he was purchased by the Boston Red Sox and, as a 27-year-old

124

Gavvy Cravath (center) sits with teammates Casey Stengel (left) and Fred Luderus in a 1919 game. *Courtesy of Getty Images*

rookie, he became the first player from the San Diego area to play in the major leagues.

Although he was batting a respectable .256 with 11 triples in 94 games, the Red Sox were dissatisfied with Cravath's lack of speed and sold him to the Chicago White Sox.

"They call me Wooden Shoes and Piano Legs and a few other pet names," Cravath once said. "I do not claim to be the fastest man in the world, but I can get around the bases with a fair wind and all sails set. And so long as I'm busting the old apple on the seam, I am not worrying a great deal about my legs."

But Gavvy hardly busted "the old apple" with the White Sox—batting just .180 in 19 games—and was traded to the Washington Senators. After four games with Washington in which he went hitless in six at-bats, Cravath was sent back to the minor leagues with the Minneapolis Millers of the American Association.

In Minneapolis, Cravath regained his stroke and was a key man on one of the greatest minor league teams of all time. There, he learned to hit the ball to the opposite field to take advantage of the short right-field fence in the Millers' Nicollet Park, a distance of 279 feet. That knack for hitting the ball the other way would serve him in good stead in later years when Cravath was with the Phillies.

Cravath got his second—and last—chance at the big leagues in 1912 when he joined the Phillies at the age of 31. This time he made good, batting .284 with 11 homers (tied for third in the National League and just three behind the league leader) and 70 RBIs. He also tied for the league lead in outfield assists with 26.

In Philadelphia, Cravath's career took off. In 1913 he led the league in hits with 179, home runs with 19, RBIs with 128, total bases with 298, and slugging percentage at .568; he was second in batting at .341.

Two years later he again led the league in homers with 24, 11 more than his closest competitor. He also led the league in runs, RBIs, total bases, walks, on-base percentage, slugging percentage, and outfield assists. And on August 8, he tied a major-league record with four doubles in one game. On September 29, his three-run homer helped the Phillies clinch their first pennant.

In 1918 Cravath became the first player to lead his league in home runs five times when he won the National League title with eight and, in so doing, raised his career home run total to 106, making him baseball's leading home-run hitter among active players. He supplanted the legendary Honus Wagner, who had retired that season. Cravath would hold the home-run lead among active players for two more years, the last two of his career. But by then it was apparent that Cravath would soon be replaced as reigning home-run king by a young left-handed pitcher-turned-outfielder who had recently been sold by the Boston Red Sox to the New York Yankees. That slugger, of course, was George Herman "Babe" Ruth.

The following year, at the age of 38, Cravath hit 12 home runs to lead the National League for a sixth time, setting a record that would go on to be tied by Mel Ott and then broken by Ralph Kiner and later Mike Schmidt.

Midway through that 1919 season, with the team in last place, the Phillies fired manager Jack Coombs and made Cravath their player-manager. Despite failing to improve the Phillies' position in the standings, Cravath was brought back in 1920. Again, the Phillies finished in last place, and Cravath was let go. He ended his major-league career with 117 home runs, 116 of them as a Phillie, which remained a franchise record until 1924, four years after Cravath's retirement, when it was eclipsed by Cy Williams.

It seemed Cravath had a dual personality: one as a hard-driving, hell-for-leather player and another as a manager and private citizen. He was fired as manager of the Phillies because he was deemed to be too easygoing. Years later, he was elected justice of the peace in Laguna Beach, California, but was eventually voted out of office in the face of criticism that the man once called "Cactus" was too soft.

Gene Mauch once said of **Johnny Callison**, "He can run, throw, and hit with power. There's nothing he can't do well on a ballfield."

And Callison did it all well for the Phillies for 10 seasons, the first two (1960–61) in left field, the next eight in right field.

In that 10-year span, Callison led the National League in doubles once, triples twice, outfield assists four times, and double plays by an outfielder once. He also played in three All-Star Games.

Callison signed with the White Sox out of Bakersfield [California] High School and reached Chicago in 1958 as a 19-year-old. The White Sox won the American League pennant in 1959 but left Callison off their World Series roster. After losing the World Series to the Dodgers, the White Sox believed

Johnny Callison was a standout on some less-than-stellar Phillies clubs.

127

they needed a veteran right-handed bat to put them over the top in 1960, and they settled on Phillies third baseman Gene Freese. In return, they offered Callison to the Phillies.

It was one of those typical trades of today for tomorrow. The Sox got the hitter they wanted (Freese batted .273 for the Sox with 17 homers and 79 RBIs, but the White Sox finished third anyway) and the Phillies got a young prospect who would have a productive 10-year run for them.

In a cruel twist of fate, Callison's best season with the Phillies is one of the worst years in the team's history. It happened in 1964, when the team blew a 6½-game lead with 12 games to play. But the collapse was no fault of Callison, who had some big moments that year.

Selected on the National League All-Star team, Callison did what only Hall of Famer Ted Williams and Stan Musial had done before him: hit a walkoff home run to win the game. It came against Dick Radatz in New York's Shea Stadium with two runners on in the bottom of the ninth and earned Callison the game's Most Valuable Player honors.

During the Phillies' 12-game slide at the end of the season, Callison was a respectable 12-for-48 with four home runs (three of them in one game) and 10 RBIs. For the season, Callison was third in the league with 31 homers and fifth with 104 runs batted in. He finished second to the Cardinals' Ken Boyer in the Most Valuable Player voting.

Statistical Summaries

All statistics are for player's Phillies career only.

HITTING

G = Games

H = Hits

HR = Home runs

RBI = Runs batted in

SB = Stolen bases

BA = Batting average

Right Fielder	Years	G	H	HR	RBI	SB	BA
Chuck Klein *Hit for the cycle twice (7/1/31 vs. Cubs, 5/26/33 vs. Cardinals)*	1928–33, 1936–39, 1940–44	1,405	1,705	243	983	71	.326
Sam Thompson *First left-handed batter to hit 20 homers in a season (1889)*	1889–98	1,034	1,478	95	963	192	.334
Elmer Flick *Had at least 20 assists each season with Phillies, including league-leading 23 in 1901*	1898–1901	537	683	29	377	119	.338

continued	Years	G	H	HR	RBI	SB	BA
Bobby Abreu *Had a single and walk as NL's leadoff batter in 2005 All-Star Game at Detroit*	1998–2006	1,353	1,474	195	814	254	.303
Gavvy Cravath *Had a .309 BA, .400 on-base pct., and slugging pct. of .526 between 1913–15*	1912–20	1,103	1,054	117	676	80	.291
Johnny Callison *Hit seven of his 226 career HRs against Juan Marichal, most off of any one pitcher*	1960–69	1,432	1,438	185	666	60	.271

FIELDING

PO = Putouts

A = Assists

E = Errors

DP = Double plays

TC/G = Total chances divided by games played

FA = Fielding average

Right Fielder	PO	A	E	DP	TC/G	FA
Chuck Klein	2,617	170	103	30	2.3	.964
Sam Thompson	1,572	202	109	43	1.8	.942
Elmer Flick	981	91	74	24	2.1	.935
Bobby Abreu	2,518	89	45	12	1.9	.983
Gavvy Cravath	1,547	169	98	25	1.8	.946
Johnny Callison	2,925	161	49	29	2.3	.984

NINE

P

Right-Handed Pitcher

For most people—and I'm one—when they hear Philadelphia Phillies, the first name that comes to mind is **Robin Roberts**, who not only was a great Hall of Fame pitcher but a man of class and dignity and one of the nicest guys you'd ever want to meet.

I had the good fortune to know him and to talk baseball with him and to listen to his stories about the players from his day when he came to Clearwater for spring training or when he visited Philadelphia occasionally and spent time around the Phillies. Being with him was always a joy, and his presence in Philadelphia made it seem like a dignitary was in our midst, one with all the trappings of royalty but none of the ego.

Too many guys who achieved what Roberts did are unapproachable. Not

1. ROBIN ROBERTS

2. PETE ALEXANDER

3. JIM BUNNING

4. ROY HALLADAY

5. CURT SCHILLING

Robin. It didn't matter who you were, he treated everybody the same. He was so down to earth, you'd never know he won 286 games, made the All-Star team seven times, pitched 45 shutouts, completed 305 games, won 20 games or more six consecutive years (1950–55), and led the league in wins four times, strikeouts twice, and complete games five times.

Robin Roberts was as good as it gets on the mound.

It surprised me to learn that Roberts never won the Cy Young Award; then I found out that they didn't begin giving out the award until 1956, the year after Robin's streak of six consecutive 20-win seasons.

Here are a few more of Roberts' remarkable achievements:

- He won 234 games as a Phillie, even though the team had only four winning seasons in his 14 years with them. In that span, Roberts had a winning percentage of .5404; the remainder of the Phillies pitchers had a winning percentage of .4561.
- He pitched more than 300 innings in six consecutive years, 1950–55.
- He had a streak in which he completed 29 consecutive starts.
- He holds the record for the most consecutive Opening Day starts with the same team, 12 for the Phillies.

One record Roberts was *not* proud of was giving up 505 home runs in his career, the second most all-time. Teammates, friends, managers, and coaches kept urging him to throw inside to hitters, even knock them down if need be, but Robin would hear none of it. He was too proud and too gentle to go headhunting. But it's also worth noting that of the 505 homers he yielded, 331 of them came with nobody on base.

It was almost baseball's loss and basketball's gain when Roberts attended Michigan State to play round ball, won three varsity letters, and was team captain of the Spartans in two separate seasons. After his sophomore season, Roberts went out for the baseball team on a lark. And when the coach lamented his team's lack of pitching (a common complaint of all coaches and managers), Robin, in a gesture meant to give the coach some help, became a pitcher, and a Hall of Fame career was launched.

In 1950, his second full major-league season, Roberts became the Phillies' first 20-game winner since Grover Cleveland Alexander in 1917, Roberts' 20th win coming on the final day of the season, a 10-inning complete-game 4–1 victory over the Dodgers in Brooklyn that clinched the Phillies first pennant in 35 years. In the World Series against the Yankees, Roberts started Game 2 against Allie Reynolds and again pitched a complete game, also in 10 innings. But this time, he took a heartbreaking 2–1 defeat.

The Phillies cut ties with Roberts after the 1961 season, selling him to the Yankees. But before he even got a chance to pitch for the Yankees, he was released and picked up by the Baltimore Orioles. He won 42 games for the

The following year he was sent to the Syracuse Stars of the Class B New York State League, where he won 29 games, pitched 15 shutouts, and caught the eye of the Phillies, who purchased Alexander's contract for the bargain price of $750.

Old Pete promptly became not only the ace of the Phillies staff but the National League's best pitcher. As a rookie in 1911 he led the league in wins with 28, complete games with 31, innings pitched with 367, and shutouts with seven.

After winning 19 and 22 games respectively in the next two seasons, Alexander led the NL in wins for four straight years—from 1914–17—with 27, 31, 33, and 30 wins. He also led the league all four years in complete games with 32, 36, 38, and 34; in innings with 355, 376⅓ , 389, and 388; and strikeouts with 214, 241, 167, and 200. He led in shutouts in 1915 with 12, 1916 with 16, and 1917 with eight, and led in earned-run average in 1915 with 1.22 and 1916 with 1.55.

Because of such spectacular numbers, Old Pete is usually mentioned among the top 10 pitchers in any discussion rating baseball's greatest pitchers. Why, then, you may ask, is he not No. 1 on my list of the greatest right-handed pitchers in Phillies history? Simple. Alexander was a Phil for only eight seasons and won 190 games for them. With 14 years and 234 wins in a Philadelphia uniform, my No. 1 guy, Robin Roberts, is more closely identified with the Phillies than is Alexander. To my mind, Roberts, along with Richie Ashburn and Mike Schmidt, are the greatest heroes in Phillies history.

Alexander's Phillies career was cut short in 1918 when he was traded to the Cubs with catcher Bill Killefer for two players and $55,000. Alex won 128 games for the Cubs, including a league-leading 27 in 1920. On June 22, 1926, he was selected off the waiver wire by the St. Louis Cardinals, where he had what arguably is his most memorable moment at age 39.

It came in the 1926 World Series against the New York Yankees. Old Pete had started two games for the Cards and won them both, a 6–2 complete-game four-hitter in Game 2 and a 10–2 complete-game eight-hitter in Game 6 that knotted the Series at three games apiece. After that victory, Alexander, as was his wont, celebrated into the wee hours. He arrived at Yankee Stadium for the next day's climactic seventh game not expecting to pitch and in no shape to do so if he was asked.

With the Cardinals leading 3–2, the Yankees rallied against Jesse Haines in the bottom of the seventh, and Cards manager Rogers Hornsby sent Alexander to the bullpen. With two outs, Haines walked Lou Gehrig to load the bases. With the Yankees' rookie sensation Tony Lazzeri due up, Hornsby went to the mound to remove Haines and signaled for Alexander.

Alexander, the ageless wonder, presumably slightly hungover, nonetheless fired four knee-high fastballs and struck out Lazzeri to strand three runners. He then retired the Yankees in order in the eighth and got Earle Combs and Mark Koenig to ground out in the ninth. That brought up Babe Ruth and, pitching carefully, Alexander walked the mighty Bambino.

With the powerful Bob Meusel at bat representing the winning run and the even more powerful Gehrig on deck, Ruth inexplicably took off for second base and was gunned down by catcher Bob O'Farrell to end the game and the World Series.

A baseball player named for one United States president was depicted in the movies by another United States president.

For his heroics, the Cardinals awarded Alexander for the 1927 season with his richest contract, $17,500, and in turn the 40-year-old Alex rewarded the Cardinals with 21 wins, his highest win total in four seasons with the team.

Alexander won 16 games for the Cards in 1928 and nine in 1929. It was clear that age—and alcohol—had caught up with him, but the Phillies nonetheless saw an opportunity to bring Alex the Great back home and acquired him in a trade before the 1930 season. Unfortunately, Alex was done. He appeared in nine games, started three, and posted a record of 0–3. On May 28 he called it a career. Eight years later, he was inducted into the National Baseball Hall of Fame.

Alexander passed away in 1950. Two years after that, he was memorialized with the release of a movie about his life titled *The Winning Team*. Starring in the role of Grover Cleveland Alexander is a young actor named Ronald Reagan. Thus, a baseball player born in Nebraska named for one United States president was depicted in the movies by another United States president.

Jim Bunning's life and career are marked by a series of highlights and historical achievements. He was:

- the first pitcher since Cy Young to win 100 games and strike out 1,000 batters in each major league (Bunning won 118 games and struck out 1,406 batters for Detroit in the American League and won 106 games and struck out 1,149 batters for Philadelphia, Pittsburgh, and Los Angeles in the National League).

137

Jim Bunning put up huge numbers in his career but sadly never pitched in the big game, the World Series.

138

- second to Walter Johnson in strikeouts with 2,855 when he retired after the 1971 season.
- author of the seventh perfect game in baseball history.
- the fifth pitcher in the American League and 10th in the major leagues to strike out three batters in an inning on nine pitches.
- the seventh pitcher with both a no-hitter and a perfect game.
- the only pitcher ever to strike out Ted Williams three times in one game.
- the first (and so far only) major-league player to be elected to the United States Senate (Sen. James Paul David Bunning R-Ky. served from 1999 to 2011).

On the mound, Bunning was a notoriously fierce competitor. Thought by some to be a headhunter (while pitching for the Phillies, he led the National League in hit batters four straight seasons), his sidearm delivery was especially effective against right-handed batters. The first nine years of his 17-year major-league career were spent in Detroit. There he pitched his no-hitter, made the All-Star team five times, and had his only 20-win season in 1957 (he would win 19 games in four other seasons, one in Detroit and three in Philadelphia). But it was with the Phillies that Bunning gained the most recognition.

*A*lmost half a century after the event and nearing the end of his first term as a U.S. Senator from Kentucky, Jim Bunning reflected on his most memorable day in baseball, his perfect game against the New York Mets in 1964.

"As the game went on," he recalled, "all the pitches were working well. The slider, curve, and fastball all got thrown to the areas I was trying to throw them to. I was ahead of all the hitters, which also made it much easier."

Thumbing his nose at superstition, Bunning was talking a blue streak through the late innings of the game.

"He was jabbering like a magpie," said Gus Triandos, who caught the perfect game.

"He was coming back to the dugout, yelling at the guys and counting out the outs," remembered Phillies manager Gene Mauch.

"I didn't care about superstitions," Bunning said. "It was important to me to relax."

With two outs in the ninth, on the brink of history as Mets backup catcher John Stephenson prepared to bat as a pinch-hitter for pitcher Tom Sturdivant, Bunning beckoned Triandos to the mound.

"He wanted me to tell him a joke," said Triandos incredulously. "But I couldn't think of anything."

Five pitches later, Stephenson was Bunning's 10th strikeout victim and the perfect game was complete but not forgotten.

"The perfect game continued to follow me in that people kept reminding me of it," Bunning said. And in case it ever strayed too far from his mind, another constant and not-so-subtle reminder came on June 21, 1997, exactly 33 years after his big day, with the birth of James Lewis Bunning, his grandson.

Bunning had followed up a 19–10 season with the Tigers in 1962 by slipping to 12–13 and, although he was still only 32 years old, he was traded to the Phillies in a four-player deal. In Philly, Bunning went immediately to the head of the class, the ace of a staff that included Chris Short, Art Mahaffey, Ray Culp, and Dallas Green.

In 1964 to 1966, his first three years as a Phillie, Bunning was remarkably consistent. He won 19 games each year; had earned-run averages of 2.63, 2.60, 2.41; pitched 284⅓, 291, 314 innings; struck out 219, 268, 252 batters; and pitched five, seven, and five shutouts.

On June 21, 1964, in the first game of a doubleheader against the Mets in New York's Shea Stadium, Bunning pitched the major league's seventh perfect game and the first in the National League in 84 years. It came on Father's Day, which brought widespread attention to Bunning, at the time the father of eight (the Bunnings would later welcome a ninth child).

Switching from one league to another is not easy, but Halladay made the transition smoothly.

While the 1964 season was such a personal triumph for Bunning on so many levels, the season's ending was a disaster. On September 13, Bunning went the distance on a seven-hitter to beat the Giants 4–1 in 10 innings and improve his record to 17–4. The Phillies were six games in front in the National League.

Over the next 17 days, during which the Phillies were sucked under by a 10-game losing streak and watched their lead slowly melt away, Bunning made six starts and lost four of them. Three times he started with only two days' rest and lost all three. Bunning finished the season with 19 wins and he finished his Hall of Fame career without ever having pitched in a World Series.

Roy "Doc" Halladay is a throwback—a pitcher who hates it when he doesn't finish what he starts. That's why in a five-year stretch from 2007 to 2011, with two teams in two leagues, he led all pitchers with 42 complete games.

If you don't think 42 complete games is a lot, consider this: In 2007 Halladay had more complete games than 26 major league *teams*. In 2008 he had more than 28 teams; 26 in 2009; 25 in 2010; and 24 in 2011.

With all those complete games and an average of 19 wins a season, Doc is not only a stud at the top of the rotation and a staff leader but makes the rest of the starters better and saves wear and tear on the bullpen. And because he's such a dedicated and tireless worker, his work ethic makes him a great role model for the other pitchers on the staff, especially the young ones.

Halladay had already put up excellent numbers in 12 seasons with the Toronto Blue Jays—22 wins in 2003, a Cy Young Award, six All-Star Games—when the Phillies got him in a trade in December 2009. Halladay was approaching free agency and it was apparent that the Blue Jays were not going to be able to sign him, so there was a rush of teams bidding to get him in a trade. The Phillies won out by offering three prospects, and the Blue Jays accepted, a tribute to the Phillies' abundant farm system.

Switching from one league to another is not easy, especially for a pitcher who often depends on his knowledge of the hitters he faces so frequently. But Halladay made the transition smoothly.

In his first season in Philadelphia Doc led the National League with 21 wins (the most by a Phillie since Steve Carlton in 1982 and the most by a right-handed Phillie since Robin Roberts in 1955), nine complete games, and four shutouts. He made the All-Star team and was the unanimous winner of the Cy Young Award, joining Roger Clemens, Pedro Martinez, Randy Johnson, and Gaylord Perry as the only players to win the Cy Young in each league. He pitched the 20th perfect game in major-league history against the Florida Marlins on May 29, 2010, and later, in Game 1 of the National League Division Series against the Cincinnati Reds, joined Johnny Vander Meer,

Roy Halladay is a complete-game pitcher, an anomaly in today's world of pitch counts and relievers.

Allie Reynolds, Virgil Trucks, and Nolan Ryan as the only men to pitch two no-hitters during the same calendar year.

After such a short time, Halladay jumps in on my all-time Phillies list at No. 4 among right-handed pitchers with a bullet, as they say in the recording industry. So look out below, Robin Roberts, Grover Cleveland Alexander, and Jim Bunning; Doc Halladay is gunning for you.

Curt Schilling's legacy always will be "the bloody sock." It came in Yankee Stadium on October 19, 2004, in the ALCS, and it came coincidentally and fittingly when Schilling was a member of the Boston Red Sox.

In order to pitch Game 6, with the Yankees leading the series 3–2, Schilling had undergone a surgical procedure on his ankle. During the game, the injured area began to bleed, saturating his sanitary sock with blood. It was all there for a national television audience to see. Schilling pitched into

Curt Schilling is best known for his World Series play with Boston and Arizona, but he was deadly in Philadelphia, too.

the eighth inning in a 4–2 Red Sox victory that tied the Series. The Red Sox would win Game 7 and then capture their first World Series in 86 years.

The incident validated Schilling as a relentless competitor and a big-game pitcher that he had exhibited several times over in his career.

Schilling was originally signed by the Red Sox in 1986. Before he could reach Boston, he was traded first to the Orioles and then to the Astros. He won four games and lost 11 in parts of four seasons when he was traded to Philadelphia. With the Phillies, he first attracted attention by winning 30 games in two seasons, establishing his reputation as a big-game pitcher.

In the '93 National League Championship Series against the Atlanta Braves, Schilling started Games 1 and 5, pitched eight innings in each without a decision, and the Phillies won each game in 10 innings by identical scores of 4–3. The Phillies then took Game 6 to advance to the World Series and Schilling was named Most Valuable Player of the NLCS.

Schilling was the losing pitcher in Game 1 of the World Series against the Toronto Blue Jays but came back in Game 5, with the Phillies down three games to one, and shut out the Jays on five hits, 2–0. Toronto won Game 6 to clinch the series.

Schilling went on to win 101 games in nine seasons with the Phillies, who traded him to the Arizona Diamondbacks midway through the 2006 season.

In Arizona, Schilling teamed with Randy Johnson to form one of the most formidable lefty-righty, one-two pitching tandems in baseball history. Together in 2001 and 2002 they combined to pitch 1,025⅔ innings and eight shutouts, strike out 1,315 batters, and win 90 games.

In the 2001 NLCS Schilling won Game 3 5–1 on a complete-game four-hitter. In the World Series against the Yankees, he won Game 1 and did not get a decision in Game 4, each time pitching seven innings, and allowing three hits. Schilling started Game 7 on three days' rest and left after seven and a third innings trailing 2–1, but the Diamondbacks rallied for two in the bottom of the ninth to win the World Series.

When he slipped to 8–9 in 2003, the Diamondbacks traded Schilling to the Red Sox. Back with the team that first signed him as an amateur free agent, Schilling won 22 games in 2004 and, bloody sock and all, led the Sox to the world championship that had eluded them for almost a century.

Statistical Summaries

All statistics are for player's Phillies career only.

PITCHING

G = Games

W = Games won

L = Games lost

PCT = Winning percentage

SHO = Shutouts

SO = Strikeouts

ERA = Earned-run average

Right-Handed Pitcher	Years	G	W	L	PCT	SHO	SO	ERA
Robin Roberts *Unofficially saved 24 games in 27 chances with Phillies*	1948–61	529	234	199	.540	35	1,871	3.46
Pete Alexander *Pitched complete game victories in both ends of doubleheader, 9/23/16 vs. Reds*	1911–17, 1930	338	190	91	.676	61	1,409	2.18

continued	Years	G	W	L	PCT	SHO	SO	ERA
Jim Bunning *Led NL in hit batsmen four consecutive years, 1964–67*	1964–67, 1970–71	226	89	73	.549	23	1,197	2.93
Roy Halladay *Entering 2012, his 20 shutouts are most of any active pitcher*	2010–11	65	40	16	.714	5	439	2.40
Curt Schilling *Held Braves and Blue Jays batters to .214 average in four post-season starts in 1993*	1992–2000	242	101	78	.564	14	1,554	3.35

FIELDING

PO = Putouts

A = Assists

E = Errors

DP = Double plays

TC/G = Total chances divided by games played

FA = Fielding average

Right-Handed Pitcher	PO	A	E	DP	TC/G	FA
Robin Roberts	238	485	19	36	1.4	.974
Grover Cleveland Alexander	113	685	15	18	2.4	.982
Jim Bunning	90	177	12	7	1.2	.957
Roy Halladay	28	70	2	0	1.5	.980
Curt Schilling	89	172	9	9	1.1	.967

TEN

Left-Handed Pitcher

Several people whose baseball knowledge and opinions I respect greatly have told me that the greatest single-season performance of any pitcher in baseball history was by **Steve Carlton** for the Phillies in 1972.

At first, I was skeptical. That year, Carlton won 27 games (many pitchers have won more than 30 in a season and one guy, Jack Chesbro, won 41 games way back in 1904), had a winning percentage of .730 (Greg Maddux, Randy Johnson, Ron Guidry and Lefty Grove all are among many pitchers who had a better winning percentage for a season), an ERA of 1.97 (in 1968 Bob Gibson had an ERA of 1.12), eight shutouts (Grover Cleveland Alexander once pitched 16 shutouts in a season), and 310 strikeouts (Nolan Ryan struck out more than 310 batters five times in his career).

1. STEVE CARLTON

2. CHRIS SHORT

3. CLIFF LEE

4. CURT SIMMONS

5. COLE HAMELS

But the more I studied Carlton's season and the more I thought about it, the more I became a believer. Carlton indeed might have had the greatest season for a pitcher in 1972. What he did was phenomenal. Here's why.

Steve Carlton's 1972 season was unbelievable.

The 1972 Phillies finished last in the National League East, 37½ games out of first place. They scored 3.1 runs per game and won only 59 games. Carlton won a remarkable 46 percent of those games. No other pitcher in baseball history ever won close to as many of his team's games. Carlton also pitched 70 percent of his team's complete games, 62 percent of their shutouts, and recorded 33 percent of their strikeouts.

His record was 5–6 when Carlton went on an incredible 18-game stretch without losing (he won 15 and had three no-decisions). In that span of two and a half months, Carlton pitched 155 innings, allowed 28 runs, and struck out 140. From July 23 to August 13, he pitched six complete-game victories, allowed just one earned run, and threw four shutouts.

TIM McCARVER: When I was released by the Red Sox in 1975, I ended up back in Philadelphia. Steve Carlton had three below-par years, and the Phillies were in a quandary. They had no idea what was wrong with him.

One night they called a meeting. In attendance were catchers Bob Boone and Johnny Oates, pitching coach Ray Rippelmeyer, manager Danny Ozark, owner Ruly Carpenter, and me. Everybody got a chance to sound off on what they thought Carlton's problem was—and everyone except Rippelmeyer and me were convinced that he wasn't throwing his fastball enough.

I said, "I'll probably be voted down here, but I played against Lefty and I played with him in St. Louis when he developed the slider and, to me, he's not throwing the slider enough."

As I predicted, I was voted down. Only Rippelmeyer kind of agreed with me, only not vociferously. But after the meeting Ray came up to me and said, "I've been saying that he wasn't throwing the slider enough but they want him to keep setting hitters up with that fastball."

I told Rippelmeyer "If I ever catch him, I'm calling for his slider, I guarantee you that." I felt strongly about it because I remembered when I played against him hitters would come back to the dugout after making out and say, "Well at least he didn't throw me the slider."

As fate would have it, I ended up catching Carlton some in 1975, but more in 1976, and I called for that wicked slider a lot. I've kidded about it ever since. I said that for the next four years I had to shake hands with three fingers.

[In four seasons with McCarver as his personal catcher, Carlton won 77 games and his second Cy Young Award.]

Carlton won six more games in 1972 than the league runner-up Tom Seaver, struck out 61 more batters than Seaver, and completed seven more games than Ferguson Jenkins. Two of Carlton's 10 losses were shutouts, and many more were squeakers: he lost two games 2–1, one 3–1, and another 3–2. Needless to say, he was the unanimous winner of the Cy Young Award, rare for a pitcher from a last place team.

The 1972 season was Carlton's first as a Phillie, and he had something to prove. He had signed with the Cardinals and, teaming with Bob Gibson to form a devastating righty-lefty, one-two punch, he helped the Birds win the 1967 and 1968 pennants. In 1969 he started and won the All-Star Game, and in a game against the Mets he set a major-league record (since broken) of 19 strikeouts, but ended up the losing pitcher. In 1971 Carlton won 20 games for the Cardinals and held out for a $10,000 raise for $65,000, which angered the owner Gussie Busch. Summarily, he ordered Carlton traded.

[Carlton was] the last major-leaguer to pitch more than 300 innings.

Shame on the Cardinals for trading Carlton and kudos to the Phillies for making what would become perhaps their best trade ever. To be fair, at the time the trade looked like an even swap, left-hander Carlton for right-hander Rick Wise, two of the best young pitchers in the National League. Wise, 26 years old, and with a career record of 75–76, was coming off a 17-win season; Carlton, nine months older, and with a career record of 77–72, was coming off a 20-win season.

Wise would go on to win 113 more games and Carlton would 242, three more Cy Young Awards, retire with the second-most strikeouts (behind Nolan Ryan), and the second-most wins for a left-hander (behind Warren Spahn). At his peak, Carlton was so dominant that when he was scheduled to pitch, the folks in Philadelphia called it "Winday."

Great pitchers like Carlton have egos. They don't like to be told how to pitch. There's a famous story about when Carlton was pitching and Willie McGee of the Cardinals was coming to bat in a critical situation. Phillies manager Paul Owens went to the mound and told Steve not to throw McGee a curve ball. So Carlton threw three curveballs in a row. *Whiff. Whiff. Whiff.* He struck out McGee practically before Owens got back to the bench. In effect, Carlton was saying, *You don't tell me what to throw.* When you have that type of player, he takes the bull by the horns. All the manager has to do is sit there.

A little-known record held by Carlton is his career 144 runners picked off base—almost twice as many as any other pitcher. However, Carlton has said that the record he's most proud of is pitching 20 years without going on the disabled list.

In many ways, Carlton, called "Lefty" by his teammates and friends, was the last of a breed. The change in pitching philosophy (pitch counts, relief specialists such as closers and setup men) seemed to begin at about the time Carlton retired in 1988. He was the last National League pitcher to win at least 25 games in a season and the last major-leaguer to pitch more than 300 innings.

Carlton's almost career-long feud with the media is well known and an unfair depiction of a man who had such a great career. Lefty had some unusual training habits (one was plunging his fist and twisting it in a five gallon bucket of rice) that were called into question by some writers. Angered by the criticism, Carlton vowed never to talk to the writers—and he never did. Carlton's silence prompted one writer to observe in 1981, when Mexican left-hander Fernando Valenzuela of the Los Angeles Dodgers broke into the big leagues with a flourish, "The two best pitchers in the National League don't speak English: Fernando Valenzuela and Steve Carlton."

Chris Short gets an unfair rap for his role in the Phillies' great fold-up of 1964. He made five starts in the last two weeks of the season and failed to win a single game—he lost two and had three no-decisions—but don't blame Short. *He* wasn't the one who made the decision to start him in four games in 11 days.

On September 14, 1964, in Houston, Short beat the Astros 4–1 with a complete-game four-hitter. It boosted his season record to 17–7 (and the 17 wins tied Short for fourth in the National League behind the Cubs' Larry Jackson and the Dodgers' Sandy Koufax and Don Drysdale). The Phillies sat at 87-57, leading the Cardinals by 6½ games, seven in the losing column, with 18 games to play.

A few days later, the Phillies went south. Short's next start was in Los Angeles on September 18. He left for a pinch-hitter in the eighth with the score tied 3–3. The Phillies lost 4–3 when the Dodgers scored a run in the bottom of the ninth.

In Short's next start, four days later, he was pounded by the Reds for six runs in 4⅔ innings. The Phillies lost 9–2. Short's next start came three days later against Milwaukee. He pitched into the eighth and left trailing 2–1. The Phillies ultimately lost 7–5 in 12 innings. Short pitched again with two days' rest in St. Louis on September 28. He left in the sixth inning trailing 3–0. The Phillies lost again, 5–1, their eighth-straight loss. They had tumbled into third place, a game and a half behind the Reds.

Chris Short was all-but-invincible in 1964. *Courtesy of Getty Images*

Short's last start of the season came four days later in Cincinnati. He left in the seventh inning trailing 3–0 and got a no-decision when the Phils rallied for four in the eighth to beat the Reds 4–3 and keep their slim pennant hopes alive. The Phils won the final game of the season but could not catch the Cardinals, who clinched the pennant.

The 1964 debacle always comes up when Short's name is mentioned. The fact is, from that ill-fated 1964 season through 1968, Short was among the best pitchers in a pitching-rich era that included Hall of Famers Bob Gibson, Juan Marichal, Sandy Koufax, Don Drysdale, Whitey Ford, Gaylord Perry, Tom Seaver, Steve Carlton, Hoyt Wilhelm, Warren Spahn, Jim Palmer, Nolan Ryan, Robin Roberts, Ferguson Jenkins, Catfish Hunter, and Short's own teammate Jim Bunning.

In that five-year stretch, Short won 83 games, made the All-Star team twice, and had a 20-win season in 1966. A bad back ended Short's career prematurely. He wound up with a winning record, 135–132, with 132 of his wins coming as a Phillie. The mark places him fourth on their all-time list behind three Hall of Famers, Carlton, Roberts, and Grover Cleveland Alexander.

It hasn't taken **Cliff Lee** long to zoom all the way up to No. 3 on my list of left-handed pitchers in Phillies history, and even at that I may be short-changing him (although he's not quite ready to challenge Steve Carlton for the No. 1 spot).

My decision to make Lee No. 3 is based only on a season and a half plus one sensational postseason in a Phillies uniform—but that was certainly enough to get my attention. This guy has the heart of a lion, and that's not something I'd say about a lot of pitchers. One of the things I regret is that I never got to play with him on the mound.

In 2011 he pitched six shutouts when the rest of the pitchers in the National League pitched only 30 combined and no other National League pitcher had more than two. Lee won only 17 games, but he could have won 20 with a little more offensive support. The Phillies were shut out in three of his losses and scored only one run in another.

In one game against the Marlins late in the season, Cliff was leading 1–0, one out away from a seventh shutout, when Jose Lopez tied the score with a home run. Lee was removed from the game after the ninth inning. Not only did Lee stay on the bench and watch the Phillies win the game in the tenth, but he went on the postgame show and took full responsibility for making a bad pitch to Lopez that cost him the win.

In some ways, Lee reminds me of Steve Carlton. Like Carlton, Lee doesn't like walking guys. Those pitchers believe in their ability. They come at you. Good pitchers like Carlton and Lee don't like pitching over the heart of the plate. They know when they do, they get hit hard.

After he was drafted by the Baltimore Orioles and refused to sign, Lee wound up signing with the Montreal Expos, who took him in the fourth round of the 2000 amateur draft. Two years later, the Expos, sensing the need to field a championship team in order to avoid being contracted out of baseball, made one of the worst trades in baseball history. They sent Lee, along with Grady Sizemore and Brandon Phillips, to the Indians in exchange for Bartolo Colon.

Colon won 10 games for the Expos, who finished in second place and eventually moved to Washington. Meanwhile, Lee flourished in Cleveland. From 2004 to 2006, he won 46 games for the Indians, but had a setback in 2007 when he strained his right abdominal muscle in spring training and had to be sent back to the minor leagues. Lee returned to have a spectacular 2008 season, leading the American League with 22 wins, a .880 winning percentage (22–3), and a 2.54 earned-run average, while allowing only .5 home runs and 1.4 walks per game. He also won the Cy Young Award. The following year he got off to a bad start and was traded to the Phillies for four prospects.

In Philadelphia, Lee won seven games, lost only four, and helped the Phillies reach the World Series by pitching spectacularly in the postseason. He won Game 1 of the division series, a complete-game six-hitter, 5–1 over the Colorado Rockies and beat the Dodgers in Game 3 of the NLCS, pitching eight innings, allowing three hits, and striking out 10 in an 11–0 victory.

Chosen to start Game 1 of the World Series, Lee was again superb in a complete-game, six-hit, 10-strikeout victory over the Yankees. He came back in Game 5 to beat the Yankees again, his fourth victory without a defeat in the postseason. But the Phils lost the Series four games to two.

Despite his success, on December 16, 2009, the Phillies traded Lee to the Seattle Mariners on the day they had acquired Roy Halladay in a trade with the Toronto Blue Jays. The Phillies believed they did not have sufficient coin to afford both Halladay and Lee.

Much-traveled Cliff Lee is thriving again in Philadelphia.

Midway through the 2010 season, with Lee facing free agency, the Mariners traded him to the Texas Rangers. Again, Lee found himself in the postseason and again he pitched brilliantly…until the World Series. He won Games 1 and 5 of the division series against Tampa Bay, allowing two runs and striking out 21, and pitched eight innings allowing two hits and striking out 13 in an 8–0 victory over the Yankees in Game 3 of the ALCS to run his postseason record to 7–0. But he lost two games to the Giants in the World Series and took the plunge into free agency.

For weeks it was rumored that Lee had narrowed his choices down to two, the Texas Rangers and New York Yankees. The Yankees, in fact, had offered him the most lucrative deal: seven years for $148 million. But Lee shocked the baseball world by turning down both the Yankees and Rangers and accepting less money, $120 million for five years, to sign with the Phillies— one of the few times the wealthy Yankees didn't get their man. Lee explained that, "I never wanted to leave [the Phillies] in the first place."

Nobody's going to have to hold a benefit for Lee, of course, but how rare is it in this day for a player to leave money on the table? Lee could have signed with the Yankees for more money or with the Rangers to be closer to his home in Arkansas, but he chose to go where he felt most comfortable. When a pitcher goes to a team that plays in a place known as a hitter's ballpark, like Philadelphia's Citizen Bank Park, and to a team where he figured to play second fiddle to Roy Halladay, you have to admire his commitment, loyalty, and his self-confidence.

Character! The guy gets it. He has character. He's not someone who cares about being No. 1. None of the Phillies pitchers do—not Lee, not Roy Halladay, not Cole Hamels, and not Roy Oswalt. My hat's off to them all. That's what makes them compatible. They like each other, they're stoic, they never complain, and they pull for one another all while being competitive against one another.

The Phillies' starting pitchers had this thing going in 2011 where they competed among each other on offense for which of them got the most hits, the most sacrifices, and so on. That's another competitive thing that Lee embraced. Among the Phillies' starting pitchers, he had the most hits, the most RBIs, and he hit the pitching corps' only two home runs.

It's rare that a team gets a second bite at the apple (in this case the Big Apple), but as they entered the 2011 season with a pair of aces in Lee and Halladay, the Phillies had their cake and ate it, too.

Curt Simmons was a homegrown product and one of the first of baseball's so-called "bonus babies."

Born in Egypt, Pennsylvania, a dot on the map in Whitehall Township, Lehigh County, some 10 miles north of Allentown and 100 miles northwest of Philadelphia, Simmons caught the Phillies' eye as a teenager in the late 1940s when he led Whitehall High to three straight league championships. His stellar play prompted team owner Bob Carpenter to arrange an exhibition game in 1947 between his Phillies and an All-Star team of high school players from the Lehigh Valley.

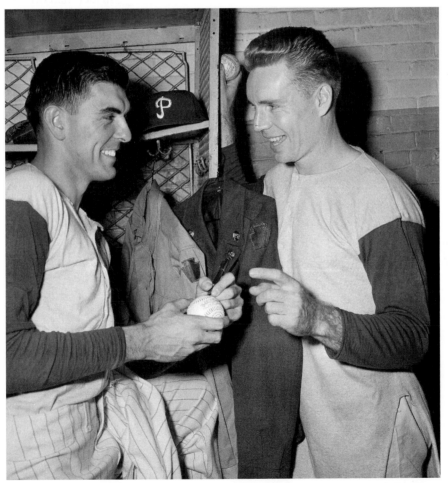

Curt Simmons (left) signs a ball for pitcher Jocko Thompson after returning on furlough from military service in 1950.

The game was played to commemorate the opening of Egypt Memorial Park before a crowd of 4,500 who were in awe (as were the Phillies) when the game ended in a 4–4 tie and young Simmons struck out 11 Phillies.

That spring, Simmons also pitched and played the outfield in an All-American high school game between teams managed by Babe Ruth and Ty Cobb.

So taken with Simmons was Carpenter that he signed the 18-year-old left-hander to a contract calling for $65,000, one of the highest bonuses ever paid a baseball player at a time when there was no free agency, no agents, and before salaries skyrocketed.

[Hamel's] 2008 had been good, but nothing that foretold what was to come.

Simmons began his professional career in 1947 with Wilmington in the Class B Interstate League where he won 13 games and lost only five. That earned him a promotion to the Phillies for a look in September. He made his major-league debut in the second game of a doubleheader against the Giants in New York's Polo Grounds on September 28, the final day of the 1947 season. Simmons struck out nine Giants and won the game 3–1 with a complete-game five-hitter. He remained with the Phillies to stay for the next 13 years.

158

Control problems afflicted Simmons as he won only 11 games and lost 23 over the next two seasons, but it all came together for him in 1950 when he combined with Robin Roberts to give the Phillies a potent one-two starting punch. He had won 17 games when, in early September, with the outbreak of the Korean War, he was called into active duty by the National Guard. He spent all of 1951 in the military and returned to the Phillies to win 14 games in 1952.

Simmons' major-league career spanned 20 seasons and four teams—the Phillies, Cardinals, Cubs and Angels. He had a career record of 193–183. He's fifth on the Phillies' all-time list in wins with 115, sixth in shutouts with 18, and seventh in strikeouts with 1,052.

In 2008, when the Phillies at long last ended their 28-year drought and finally won the franchise's second World Series, Steve Carlton was long gone and Roy Halladay and Cliff Lee had not yet arrived. Somebody had to step up and lead the charge, and that somebody was a young guy, practically a baby—a California beach baby at that—named **Colbert Michael Hamels**, who wasn't even born when the Phillies had won their last World Series.

Cole Hamels has been good as gold for the Phils.

The Phillies first round pick out of San Diego's Rancho Bernardo High School in the June 2002 amateur draft, Cole Hamels was just a few months shy of his 25th birthday when the 2008 postseason began, but he had already spent three seasons in the major leagues and had won 38 games. His 2008 had been good—a record of 14–10, an earned-run average of 3.09, two shutouts, and 196 strikeouts in 227⅓ innings—but nothing that foretold what was to come.

Hamels got the ball for Game 1 of the division series against Milwaukee, allowed no runs and two hits, and struck out nine in eight innings of a 3–1 win. The Phillies won the series in four games.

In the National League Championship Series against the Los Angeles Dodgers, Hamels again started Game 1, pitched seven innings and was the winning pitcher in a 3–2 Phillies victory. He then pitched the clinching Game 5, again went seven innings, and again was the winning pitcher in a 5–1 victory that sent the Phillies to the World Series. For his efforts, Hamels was voted Most Valuable Player of the NLCS.

Hamels was on a roll, and manager Charlie Manuel named him his starting pitcher in the opening game of the World Series against the Tampa Bay Rays. It was more of the same: seven innings in the Phillies' 3–2 victory. Hamels was a perfect 4–0 in the postseason and he had won the clincher in both the NLDS and NLCS and had one more chance to win a clincher in the World Series. He started Game 5, pitched six innings, and left with the Phillies ahead 3–2. The Rays tied it in the top of the seventh, but the Phillies regained the lead in the bottom of the seventh and won 4–3. Hamels was not involved in the decision, but he was voted World Series MVP.

The Phillies didn't have Halladay in 2008, and they didn't have Lee. Hamels was the No. 1 guy. To take that responsibility on his shoulders and win the World Series was just awesome. And he did it with just two pitches, a fastball and a change-up. To demonstrate how good he is and how much of a competitor he is, Cole wasn't satisfied. He's worked to come up with a curveball and a cutter. Two new pitches! And he's still young, still learning. His future is limitless.

Statistical Summaries

All statistics are for player's Phillies career only.

PITCHING

G = Games

W = Games won

L = Games lost

PCT = Winning percentage

SHO = Shutouts

SO = Strikeouts

ERA = Earned-run average

Left-Handed Pitcher	Years	G	W	L	PCT	SHO	SO	ERA
Steve Carlton *Hit three homers and drove in 15 runs in 1977*	1972–86	499	241	161	.574	39	3,031	3.09
Chris Short *Pitched scoreless ninth and tenth innings in 1967 All-Star Game*	1959–72	459	132	127	.510	24	1,585	3.38
Cliff Lee *Has held Michael Bourn hitless in 15 career at-bats with five strikeouts through 2011*	2009, 2011	44	24	12	.667	7	312	2.65

continued	Years	G	W	L	PCT	SHO	SO	ERA
Curt Simmons *Had a 19–6 record vs. Phillies from 1960 to 1967*	1947–50, 1952–60	325	115	110	.511	18	1,052	3.66
Cole Hamels *Struck out seven batters in five innings in first major league start vs. Reds, 5/12/06*	2006–11	181	74	54	.578	4	1,091	3.39

FIELDING

PO = Putouts

A = Assists

E = Errors

DP = Double plays

TC/G = Total chances divided by games played

FA = Fielding average

Left-Handed Pitcher	PO	A	E	DP	TC/G	FA
Steve Carlton	71	488	29	21	1.2	.951
Chris Short	111	347	17	22	1.0	.964
Cliff Lee	10	38	2	2	1.1	.960
Curt Simmons	68	279	13	15	1.1	.964
Cole Hamels	49	150	6	9	1.1	.971

ELEVEN

Relief Pitcher

Imagine Mariano Rivera or Brad Lidge or Trevor Hoffman starting Game 1 of the World Series; imagine him not only starting it, but pitching eight innings, giving up only one run, and losing the game.

This preamble is by way of introducing **Jim Konstanty**, No. 1 on my list of all-time Phillies relief pitchers. I wasn't impressed by Konstanty until I heard the story of his World Series experience. That's what convinced me that he belongs on the top of the list.

Before there were pitch counts, closers, and Mariano Rivera, there was Casimir James "Jim" Konstanty, a bespectacled, professorial right-hander who was to the Phillies in their 1950 pennant season what Rivera has been to the Yankees over the past two decades.

Konstanty not only looked like an intellectual, he was one. A graduate of Syracuse University with a bachelor of science degree who started out as a physical-education teacher, he detoured to play professional baseball for 17 years, 11 in the major leagues with five different teams, and came full circle after retiring from baseball to spend six

1. Jim Konstanty

2. Steve Bedrosian

3. Tug McGraw

4. Brad Lidge

5. Jose Mesa

Jim Konstanty was brains and brawn on the mound for Philadelphia.

164

years as athletic director of Hartwick College in Oneonta, New York, some 60 miles southeast of Syracuse.

A baseball and basketball star at Syracuse, Konstanty opted for baseball and in 1941 signed with Springfield in the Class A Eastern League, where he won four games and lost 19. Nevertheless, the Cincinnati Reds presumably saw enough to purchase his contract and send Konstanty to familiar territory, Syracuse in the Double A International League.

Over the next several years, Konstanty lived a journeyman's existence, shuttling from Syracuse to Toronto in the International League and Cincinnati, Boston, and Philadelphia in the National League. He finally landed with the Phillies in 1948 at the age of 31. Along the way he gained some valuable experience and developed a palm ball. It would become his signature pitch as he made the transition from starter to reliever.

In 1949 Konstanty was the Phillies' primary reliever. The Whiz Kids were coming into their own at the time and Konstanty was a veteran presence and leader, an "old man" of the pitching staff. He appeared in 53 games, all in relief, winning nine and saving a team-high seven games (the league leader, Ted Wilks of the St. Louis Cardinals, had nine), and helped the Phillies produce their first winning season in 17 years with a team record of 81–73 and a third-place finish.

The Phillies were faced with the monumental task of trying to beat the powerful New York Yankees—and having to do it with a pitching staff that was in tatters.

A year later, the Phillies and Konstanty were the talk of the baseball world as the Phils won their first pennant in 35 years. Konstanty, pitching exclusively in relief, won 16 games and obliterated the National League record for appearances by a pitcher with 74 and saves with 22, 14 more than the league runner-up, Bill Werle of Pittsburgh.

There was no Cy Young Award in 1950 (it would not be introduced for six more years), but Konstanty easily won the Most Valuable Player Award in a landslide over Stan Musial. He was the first—and remains to this day the only—relief pitcher to win the National League MVP.

In the World Series, the Phillies were faced with the monumental task of trying to beat the powerful New York Yankees—and having to do it with a pitching staff that was in tatters. In their stretch run, Phillies ace Robin Roberts had pitched 18 innings in a period of four days. Their No. 2 starter, Curt Simmons, had been called into military service and had last pitched on September 9. Their No. 3 starter, Bob Miller, had not won a game in almost two months.

To start the World Series against the Yankees and their 21-game winner Vic Raschi, Phillies manager Eddie Sawyer gave the ball to Konstanty, who had made 133 consecutive relief appearances for the Phillies. While it was something of a surprise that Sawyer would start his relief ace in Game 1 of the World Series, it was not as much of a gamble as one might think.

In his 74 games that season, Konstanty had pitched 152 innings, or slightly more than two innings per appearance. In 41 of his 74 appearances, he had pitched at least two innings. Seventeen times he had pitched at least three innings. By contrast, in 2011, Mariano Rivera made 64 appearances and pitched a total of $61\frac{1}{3}$ innings and only once pitched more than $1\frac{1}{3}$ innings in a game.

The bulk of the late-inning relief work for the Phillies in '85 had been handled by 38-year-old Kent Tekulve, who was coming to the end of an outstanding career as a closer. He had just 14 saves for the Phillies, so manager John Felske decided to give Bedrosian a chance to be the team's closer. Bedrock took to the job like Michael Phelps took to swimming. He saved 29 games and was a major reason the Phillies improved from 75 wins to 86 and jumped from fifth place in the National League East to second in 1986. The Phillies had found themselves a closer.

When the Phillies acquired McGraw, it was something like General Robert E. Lee changing his uniform from gray to blue.

Bedrosian was even better in 1987, although the Phillies weren't. They had a losing record and fell back to fourth place. Bedrock led the league with 40 saves, including a record at the time of 13 straight, and was voted the NL Cy Young Award winner, beating out Rick Sutcliffe, Rick Reuschel, Orel Hershiser, Dwight Gooden, and Mike Scott. He even finished 16th in the NL Most Valuable Player voting, very rare for a pitcher with a fourth-place team.

Bedrock would save only 34 more games for the Phillies, but he had had his 15 minutes of fame in Philadelphia. He was traded to the Giants midway through the 1989 season.

Bedrosian, who studied criminal justice in college, once said, "I wanted to be a Massachusetts state trooper on a motorcycle." Instead, he pitched 14 seasons in the major leagues, won 76 games, saved 184 games, and made enough money to buy several motorcycles. Although he was with them for only three and a half of his 14 big league seasons, 21 of Bedrock's 76 wins, 103 of his 184 saves, and his only Cy Young Award all came with the Phillies.

Because he coined the slogan for their 1986 National League championship, **Tug McGraw** is most closely associated with the New York Mets, but the fact is, Tug spent more years (10–9), won more games (49–47) and earned more saves (94–86) with the Phillies than he did with the Mets.

Tug is a larger-than-life Philadelphia legend and idol because he threw the pitch in Game 6 of the 1980 World Series that Willie Wilson of the Kansas City Royals swung at and missed to clinch the Phillies' first world championship.

For the first nine years of his major-league career, McGraw had been a key component in the Phillies' archrival Mets' two pennants and one World Series. At the same time, in that nine-year span from 1965 to 1974, the

Tug McGraw (left) celebrates the Phils' 1983 NL pennant-winning victory.

Phillies had fallen on hard times, finishing higher than fifth place only twice. Because of the hostile relations between the Mets and Phillies, when, on December 3, 1974, the Phillies acquired McGraw from the Mets in a six-player trade, it was something like General Robert E. Lee changing his uniform from gray to blue.

The acquisition of McGraw was intended to help fortify a Phillies bullpen that had accumulated more than 27 saves only once in the previous nine years. With the addition of McGraw, his signature wicked screwball, and his 94 saves, the Phillies amassed more than 27 saves nine times in the next 10 years, four times exceeding 40 saves.

The 10 years in which McGraw was a Phil represented a reversal of fortune for the Phillies and the Mets. While the Mets failed to win a division title and finished fifth or sixth seven times in that 10-year period, the Phillies, with McGraw, were winning five division titles, two pennants, and one World Series.

Tug was already a six-year Phillies veteran when I joined the team in 1981, and he became my friend and one of my favorite teammates, a free spirit with a quick wit who loved life. That's why it was so hard to take when we learned he had a malignant brain tumor and died at the age of 59.

ug McGraw was a loose cannon, a media favorite for his quick wit and his ability and willingness to deliver a clever line for attribution. Curiously, it first came to light by accident, in 1973 when Tug was a member of the New York Mets.

On August 17 the Mets, under manager Yogi Berra, lost to the Reds 2–1 and fell to 53–66, in last place in the National League East, 7½ games behind the first-place Cardinals. After the game, the Mets were paid a visit in their clubhouse by M. Donald Grant, the team's chairman of the board, a stately and somewhat pompous Wall Street executive.

"Mr. Grant came to the locker room and gave us this pep talk," remembered Joe Pignatano, a Mets coach that season. "'You gotta believe in yourself,' he said. 'You gotta *believe* in the fellow alongside of you.' Believe, believe, believe. He kept saying *believe*. He started to leave and he was almost out the door when Tug jumped up and started shouting, 'You gotta believe, you guys. You gotta believe.' He thought Grant was gone, but he wasn't. He was still there and he heard Tug and came back into the room to see who was talking. Tug just looked at him and without missing a beat he said, 'You're right, Mr. Grant; you gotta believe.' Everybody just started shaking their heads. Here Tug was mimicking the chairman of the board and he turns it around and makes a negative into a positive."

"Tug was one of those rare individuals in the game—not to sound negative because it's actually a positive—who found enjoyment even in losing," pitcher Tom Seaver remembers. "He was that kind of effervescent and positive personality; even when he lost it was still a day at the ballpark and it was still a baseball game.

"The slapping of his glove on his thigh after getting a save; my first impression was that it was hot-dogging," Seaver continued. "He did it initially as something between him and his wife in the stands. He would come off the mound and the slapping of his glove on his thigh was a signal to his wife. Then it became something bigger, and it grew into 'You gotta believe,' and that became a rallying cry. He was mocking Grant, but he took it and used it and ran with it."

"You gotta believe" became a slogan for the 1973 Mets as they closed ground and eventually caught and passed the Cardinals to win the NL East and the National League Championship Series and got to the World Series. "You gotta believe" would be a major part of the McGraw's legacy, a legacy he would embellish as a member of the Phillies with the following choice comments:

"I have no trouble with the 12 inches between my elbow and my palm. It's the seven inches between my ears that's bent."

"Kids should practice autographing baseballs. This is a skill that's often overlooked in Little League."

Asked if he preferred grass or AstroTurf: "I don't know. I never smoked AstroTurf."

On the pitch he threw that struck out Willie Wilson of the Kansas City Royals for the final out that clinched the first World Series championship in the almost century-long history of Phillies baseball: "They say that was the slowest fastball ever thrown in Philadelphia. It took 97 years to get there."

Asked what he planned to do with the money he was to receive after signing a lucrative new contract with the Phillies: "Ninety percent I'll spend on good times, women, and Irish whiskey. The other 10 percent I'll probably waste."

Tug had made Philadelphia his adopted home and was a familiar figure in and around Philly, attending important events as a Phillies alumnus, such as the closing ceremonies at Veterans Stadium and narrating "Casey at the Bat" with the Philadelphia Pops Orchestra.

After his death, Tug was cremated. Five years later his son, superstar country and western singer Tim McGraw, took a handful of his dad's ashes and spread them on the pitcher's mound at Citizens Bank Park prior to Game 3 of the 2008 World Series.

The saga of **Brad Lidge** is one of uncommon success one year, disappointment and injury the next. When he's healthy and on the field, Lidge is one of the best closers in baseball; the problem has been keeping him healthy and on the field.

Lidge came up through the Astros' farm system as a starting pitcher but made only one start for the Astros, in 2002, then was moved to the bullpen the following year, serving as setup man to closer Billy Wagner. When

Brad Lidge has been sidelined by injury, but when he's on, he's unbeatable.

Wagner was traded to the Phillies in 2004 and Octavio Dotel was ineffective as Wagner's replacement, Lidge inherited the closer's role in Houston in July, saved 29 games, set a National League record for strikeouts by a relief pitcher with 157, and won one game and saved two while pitching eight scoreless innings and striking out 14 in the NLCS against the Cardinals.

Lidge joined the roster of elite closers in 2005 when he saved 42 games and did not allow a run in 42 of his last 50 appearances. The injury jinx hit Lidge in 2007. He missed six games with a bone bruise on his knee, 20 more with an oblique strain, and saved only 19 games. After the season, Lidge had knee surgery. While he was recuperating the Astros, presumably concerned that Lidge might not return to his previous form, acquired Jose Valverde from the Diamondbacks to be their closer and traded Lidge to the Phillies.

Lidge joined the roster of elite closers in 2005 when he saved 42 games and did not allow a run in 42 of his last 50 appearances.

In February, pitching off the mound during spring training, Lidge tore the meniscus in his right knee—the one on which he had recently had surgery—had it repaired with arthroscopic surgery, and didn't return until April 6 to start the season after missing most of spring training.

Lidge nevertheless had his greatest season in 2008, posting a 2–0 record with a 1.95 earned-run average, striking out 92 batters in 69⅓ innings and saving 41 games in 41 save opportunities. He followed that up with two saves in the division series, three saves and a 0.00 ERA in 4⅓ innings over four games in the NLCS, and two saves and an 0.00 ERA in the World Series which culminated in him getting the final out of the Series to complete his perfect season—41 saves in 41 opportunities in the regular season and seven saves in seven opportunities in the playoffs and World Series. The Phillies rewarded Lidge by signing him to a three-year extension.

Those three years brought more saves and more pitching brilliance. However, they also brought more time lost because of injury.

Jose Mesa's nickname is "Joe Table"—the literal English translation of his name—but it should be "the Wanderer." Here's a guy who had a productive 19-year major-league career, most of it as a closer, with 80 wins, 321 saves, and more than 1,000 strikeouts, and yet he bounced around to eight different teams—the Indians, Phillies, Orioles, Pirates, Mariners, Rockies, Giants, and Tigers.

Jose Mesa is still the all-time saves leader in Phillies history.

174

There are two ways to look at all that moving around. Either seven teams couldn't wait to get rid of him, or seven teams were eager to get him.

Jose actually signed his first professional contract with a ninth team, the Toronto Blue Jays, as an outfielder, but never made it to Toronto. He was traded to the Orioles and began his major-league career in Baltimore as a starting pitcher. It wasn't until his sixth major-league season, in 1994, that Mesa became a reliever and picked up the first of his 321 saves at the age of 28. The next year he led the American League with 46 saves. He would have three other seasons with at least 40 saves, two of them in succession with the Phillies, 2001 and 2002, when he saved 42 and 45 games. In 2003 he fell off to 24 saves, and the Phillies let him walk as a free agent.

The 111 saves he accumulated in three seasons, plus one he picked up when he returned to Philadelphia in 2007, the final year of his career, make Mesa the all-time saves leader in Phillies history.

Statistical Summaries

All statistics are for player's Phillies career only.

PITCHING

G = Games

W = Games won

L = Games lost

PCT = Winning percentage

SV = Saves

SO = Strikeouts

ERA = Earned-run average

Relief Pitcher	Years	G	W	L	PCT	SV	SO	ERA
Jim Konstanty *Named 1950 Athlete of the Year by the Associated Press*	1948–54	314	51	39	.567	54	205	3.64
Steve Bedrosian *Only saved one game in April of his 1987 Cy Young season*	1986–89	218	21	18	.538	103	241	3.29
Tug McGraw *Had only one losing record (2–4 in 1981) in his 10 seasons with the Phils*	1975–84	463	49	37	.570	94	491	3.10

continued	Years	G	W	L	PCT	SV	SO	ERA
Brad Lidge *Didn't allow a run in 68 of 81 appearances (including postseason) in 2008*	2008–11	214	3	11	.214	100	228	3.73
Jose Mesa *Recorded last save (8/5) and win (9/18) of career in extra innings for 2007 division champs*	2001–03, 2007	246	13	18	.419	112	188	4.05

FIELDING

PO = Putouts

A = Assists

E = Errors

DP = Double plays

TC/G = Total chances divided by games played

FA = Fielding average

Relief Pitcher	PO	A	E	DP	TC/G	FA
Jim Konstanty	36	137	8	10	0.6	.956
Steve Bedrosian	12	29	1	2	0.2	.976
Tug McGraw	33	99	8	9	0.3	.943
Brad Lidge	9	25	2	2	0.2	.944
Jose Mesa	14	31	1	0	0.2	.978

TWELVE

Manager

Charlie Manuel will surprise you! If you haven't spent much time around him you might mistake him for the proprietor of the general store in his hometown of Buena Vista, Virginia; you might think of him as a laid-back, bumbling, unsophisticated country rube, the anti–Tony La Russa–Gene Mauch–Billy Martin–Bobby Valentine–Buck Showalter–Tommy Lasorda. You'd be wrong. He's a wise, competitive, and knowledgeable baseball lifer who has won as many World Series as Martin and more pennants than Mauch, Showalter, or Valentine.

Of course the Phillies' run of recent success is due first and foremost to their players. But somebody has to put those players in a position to succeed, and that's where Manuel comes in. It's what he does and does not do with those players that sets him apart and makes him special.

1. CHARLIE MANUEL

2. DALLAS GREEN

3. GENE MAUCH

4. DANNY OZARK

5. EDDIE SAWYER

Manuel has great patience. He knows that no hitter can be successful every game and sometimes, almost to a fault, he'll keep guys in the lineup when they're slumping. He's done it with every player from Ryan Howard to Raul Ibanez, right down the line. If he likes you and you're part of his first team, you're in there. He'll keep playing you through slumps. He'll stick with his closer even if the guy is blowing saves. Things like that make you feel good if you're a player. That kind of patience and support from the manager breeds confidence in his players. They start thinking, *The manager is showing that he'll stick with me when things aren't going well. I've got to go the extra mile for him.*

[Manuel] became one of the most popular players in Japan, known to fans and teammates as Aka-Oni, *"the red devil."*

Now you have a good thing going and a recipe for Manuel's success. He has good players, he wins, and he has the patience to stay with his players through slumps. That gets around, and players want to come to the Phillies to play; it's a positive circle that fosters success.

A manager is always going to be second-guessed. It goes with the territory. He has to be thick-skinned, and he has to have the courage of his convictions, stick with his program, and not be influenced by the critics.

Charlie is not one of those managers who acts like he invented the game. He doesn't try to outthink the guy in the opposing dugout or show how much he knows. He keeps it simple and lets his players play. He rarely puts on the squeeze play. He doesn't bunt a lot. He lets his hitters do their thing. He's not afraid to put a young player in a clutch situation and give him a chance to show what he can do. Players appreciate that kind of support and confidence from their manager, and Charlie's record speaks for itself. He wins—more than any other manager in the team's long history.

Charlie made his bones in baseball as a hitting instructor with the Cleveland Indians, where he tutored and was instrumental in the success of Albert Belle, Manny Ramirez, and Jim Thome, among many others.

Manuel has always been about hitting. He knows and understands hitting and hitters. A strapping 6'4", 200-pounder, he signed as a free agent with the Minnesota Twins and came up through their farm system with the reputation of being a lefty slugger, but he fizzled when he got to Minnesota. Playing for the Twins under Billy Martin and Bill Rigney, and later for the Dodgers under Walter Alston, Manuel batted only .198, hit four home runs, and drove in 43 runs in 242 games.

His major-league career in peril, Manuel accepted an offer to play for the Yakult Swallows in Japan's Central League. It was in Japan that Charlie flourished, became the hitter everyone thought he would be, and at the same time honed the knowledge of hitting that would serve him well back home in later years.

Manuel's confidence in his players is a huge reason for his success in Philadelphia.

In a four-year span from 1977 to 1980, playing for Yakult and the Kintetsu Buffaloes of the Pacific League, Manuel batted .316, .312, .324, and .325; hit 166 homers; drove in 423 runs; and became one of the most popular players in Japan, known to fans and teammates as *Aka-Oni,* "the red devil."

When injuries shortened his playing career in Japan, Manuel returned to the U.S. to work for the Twins, first as a scout and later as a minor-league manager. He left the Twins organization to manage in the Cleveland farm system and later served two hitches as Indians hitting instructor, the second under manager Mike Hargrove. When Hargrove was fired before the 2000 season, Manuel was named to replace him. He finished second in 2000 and won the AL Central title in 2001 but lost in the division series. When the Indians got off to a 39–47 start in 2001, Manuel was let go.

He wasn't out of work long. The Phillies hired him as a special assistant to the general manager, putting him in place to take over as manager when Larry Bowa was bounced after the 2004 season.

The rest, as they say, is Philadelphia Phillies history, as Charlie has put together an impressive resume including, through the 2011 season, five consecutive National League East titles, two pennants, and one World Series title. In 2011, as the Phillies won a franchise-record 102 games, Charlie won his 646th game as manager of the Phillies, passing Gene Mauch for the most managerial wins in Phillies history. At .570 his winning percentage is better than any other Phillies manager since 1900. His overall winning percentage with the Indians and Phillies of .561 is 20th all-time and 14th since 1900, and he has a winning record in each of his nine seasons as a major-league manager.

Major-league pitcher, manager, farm director, general manager. **Dallas Green** has done it all in baseball, and then some. He even was hired and fired as a manager by George Steinbrenner, but then that hardly makes him unique. What does make him unique is that he was the Phillies' man in the dugout, their manager, in 1980 when they won the World Series and ended a drought that had lasted almost 100 years.

It's for that momentous accomplishment, that magic moment when Tug McGraw struck out Willie Wilson and the Phillies reigned supreme in baseball for the first time, that I choose Green as No. 2 on my list of all-time Phillies managers despite having held the job for only three years and having won only 169 games, fewer than 22 of the 50 other guys who have had the job.

By his own description, Dallas is a no-nonsense guy and hardly the possessor of a warm and fuzzy personality when it comes to doing his job. He once said, "I'm a screamer, a yeller, and a cusser. I never hold back."

He's never been afraid to speak his mind, even if it meant putting his job at risk. He was fired by the Yankees after sarcastically referring to Steinbrenner, the owner of the team, as "Manager George."

Dallas replaced Danny Ozark as manager of the Phillies for the final 30 games of the 1979 season. The Phillies finished that season in fourth place in the National League East, but the next year under Green they won 91 games, were division champions, and sprinted all the way to the world championship. They did all that under Green despite the fact that his gruff manner led to several clashes with some of the stars on the team.

Dallas Green's managing career in Philly was short—but very sweet.

The simple truth about Dallas is that despite his sometimes cantankerous nature, he has earned the loyalty of many of his contemporaries. Some, such as Lee Elia, John Vukovich, Pat Corrales, and John Stearns have followed him from team to team and from job to job.

Dallas gets such loyalty *from* them because he has demonstrated his loyalty *to* them.

I'm really not sure what to make of **Gene Mauch**.

His supporters—there are many and they are fervent—call him a genius as a manager, a master tactician. He advocated "small ball," using the bunt and hit-and-run to move runners along rather than waiting for the long ball. He earned a reputation for outmanaging and outthinking his opponents.

One longtime rival, Sparky Anderson, once said of Mauch: "If you had the best club, you had a chance to beat him. If he had the best club, you had no chance. If the clubs were even, he had an advantage."

Gene Mauch (right) represents the National League in the 1965 All-Star Game. His opposing manager is Al Lopez of the American League Chicago White Sox.

When he retired, Mauch had managed more games (3,942) and for more years (26) than any manager in history except Connie Mack, John McGraw, and Bucky Harris.

His detractors, on the other hand, accuse him of grossly overmanaging and point out that in 26 years he had 13 losing seasons, an overall losing record (1,902–2,037), and was the longest-tenured manager who never won a pennant.

In his playing days, Mauch had been a light-hitting infielder who batted .239 in 304 games with the Dodgers, Pirates, Cubs, Braves, Cardinals, and Red Sox and never was a starter. He spent most of his time on the bench—observing, listening, and soaking up knowledge of the game from such wily veterans as Leo Durocher, Billy Herman, Charley Grimm, Frankie Frisch, Billy Southworth, Eddie Stanky, and Mike Higgins. His first try at managing came in 1953 when, at age 27, he was named player/manager of the Atlanta Crackers, the Braves Class AA farm team in the Southern Association.

When his playing career ended, Mauch turned to managing full-time. The Red Sox made him the manager of the Minneapolis Millers, their team in the Triple A American Association, where he won 82 games in 1958 and 95 in 1959. He was set to return to the Millers in 1960, but prior to the start of the American Association season, 34-year-old Gene Mauch was chosen by the Phillies to replace Eddie Sawyer who had resigned as manager after only one game.

In his first two seasons as manager of the Phillies, Mauch lost 94 and 107 games, respectively, and endured a 23-game losing streak. He turned things around and had winning seasons in 1962–64. The 1964 season would come to define Mauch's managerial career, both the good and the bad.

"Losing streaks are funny. If you lose at the beginning, you got off to a bad start. If you lose in the middle of a season, you're in a slump. If you lose at the end, you're choking."

His Phillies won 92 games and were on the brink of winning their first pennant in 14 years when they blew a 6½ lead with 12 games to play. Mauch would never live down the collapse. He once pointedly commented: "Losing streaks are funny. If you lose at the beginning, you got off to a bad start. If you lose in the middle of a season, you're in a slump. If you lose at the end, you're choking."

When the Phillies began to decline, Mauch was let go as manager after 54 games in 1968. He wouldn't be idle long. The following year he was hired as the first manager of the expansion Montreal Expos. He suffered through a 20-game losing streak and won only 52 games that first year but improved the Expos by 27 wins in four years. But he never had a winning record in seven seasons in Montreal and was let go after the 1975 season. Again, he wasn't idle long and was hired to manage the Minnesota Twins in 1976.

After five seasons in Minnesota and still no championship, Mauch was on the move again to Southern California as manager of the Angels, where his past caught up with him. In 1982 the Angels won the American League West and took the first two games of the ALCS against the Milwaukee Brewers. Needing to win one game out of three in Milwaukee to reach the World Series, the Angels lost all three, and Mauch was denied once more.

Four years later, the Angels again won the AL West and advanced to the ALCS, now a seven-game series, against the Red Sox. The Angels won three of the first four games and were leading Game 5 5–2 in the ninth inning. Just one strike away from being eliminated, and the Angels advancing to the World Series, the Red Sox rallied for four runs, won the game, and then took the next two games to thwart the Angels and Mauch one more time. Needless to say, most reports of the ALCS made certain to mention previous collapses of teams managed by Mauch in Philadelphia and California.

It's hard to know which Gene Mauch is the real one. The people of Philadelphia, at least most of them, seem to have forgiven him for the 1964 debacle, so I will, too, and point out that until Charlie Manuel passed him, Mauch's 645 victories were the most by a Phillies manager.

It seems to me **Danny Ozark** doesn't get enough recognition for his more than 50 years in baseball as a player, coach, and manager in the minor leagues. He certainly doesn't get enough credit as a manager. There's more a tendency to portray him as a buffoon and to dwell on how he sometimes mangled the English language than to discuss his work as a manager, which was outstanding.

Ozark managed the Phillies for seven seasons and improved the team in each of his first four years on the job.

Manager Danny Ozark (right) counsels Tim McCarver before a 1977 postseason contest.

Chances are, if he had hit 358 home runs, played on 14 pennant-winners and 10 World Series champions, spent more than half a century in the game, and was voted into the Hall of Fame, Danny Ozark, and not Yogi Berra, would be considered baseball's undefeated champion of the malaprop. His supporters will stack Ozark's slips of the tongue and unintentional witticisms against Berra any day of the week and would also authenticate that the following Ozarkisms were pearls right out of the mouth of the former Phillies manager and not put there by some public-relations flack, Madison Avenue huckster, or imaginative sportswriter.

"Half this game is ninety percent mental," Ozark once said.

In May 1975 Ozark's Phillies were swept in a three-game series by the lowly Atlanta Braves, who would go on to lose 94 games that year. After the third game, Ozark told the gathered media that the sweep was "beyond my apprehension."

In the following season, Ozark watched a 15½ game lead dwindle to a mere three-game advantage. In the face of gloom and impending doom, the manager of the Phillies waxed philosophical about his team's decline. "Even Napoleon had his Watergate."

Asked if there might be a morale problem on the Phillies, Ozark responded, "This team's morality is no factor."

As the 1976 Phillies kept spinning out of control and were freefalling in the standings, general manager Paul Owens took to accompanying the team on road trips, raising speculation that Ozark's job was in jeopardy. Ozark calmly brushed aside the rumors, insisting Owens' presence "was not intimidating and, furthermore, I will not be cohorsed."

Asked to comment on reports that he had problems with his players, Ozark replied, "Contrary to popular belief, I have always had a wonderful repertoire with my players."

The Phillies righted their ship in 1976 and finished nine games ahead of the Pirates in the National League East, a tribute to their manager, who drew praise for his deft handling of the team from the writers covering the Phillies. Ozark humbly accepted the plaudits of the press with a selfless, if cryptic, comment: "Who knows what evil lurks in the hearts of men except the Shadow."

When asked by one member of the media why he never gives a straight answer, Ozark's response was as follows: "Don't you know I'm a fascist? You know, a guy who says one thing and means another."

Among Phillies managers, Ozark is fourth in wins with 594 (only Charlie Manuel, Gene Mauch, and Harry Wright have won more). At .538 he has a better winning percentage with the Phillies than Mauch, Larry Bowa, Terry Francona, Jim Fregosi, and Eddie Sawyer. His three first-place finishes in 1976, 1977, and 1978 are more than any other Phillies manager except Manuel. And until Manuel did it in 2011, Ozark was the only Phillies manager to win 100 games—and he did it twice, in back-to-back years, 1976–77, guiding a powerhouse team that included Hall of Famers Mike Schmidt and Steve Carlton to identical marks of 101–61.

Unfortunately what people remember most about Ozark's three first-place finishes is that in all three years the Phillies finished first in the National League East, they lost in the NLCS and failed to make the World Series. In 1979, with the Phillies in fourth place having lost two games more than they won, Ozark was fired and replaced by Dallas Green. The following season Green piloted the Phillies to their first World Series championship with a team in part put together by Ozark.

Ozark was a right-handed-hitting first baseman who came up through the Dodgers' farm system. He spent 18 years in the minor leagues as a player, twice hitting more than 30 home runs in a season and seven times batting .300 or better, but he never had an at-bat in the major leagues. He also managed in the minors for nine years, and his loyalty was rewarded when he was promoted to the Dodgers and served eight years as a coach under Walter Alston.

Being associated with a winning team such as the Dodgers and a Hall of Fame manager in Alston brought Ozark to the attention of the Phillies, who hired him to be their manager in 1973.

Few men that managed in the major leagues can match the résumé or the brainpower of **Eddie Sawyer**, who was a longtime minor-leaguer before he became the Phillies 32ⁿᵈ and 36ᵗʰ manager. Sawyer held a bachelor's degree from Ithaca College, where he was a member of Phi Beta Kappa, and earned a master's degree from Cornell University. Between baseball seasons, he was a science teacher.

Sawyer, no doubt aided by his experience as a teacher, had earned a reputation for being especially effective with young players.

Sawyer spent 10 years playing in the Yankees farm system, but like another Phillies manager, Danny Ozark, he never played in the major leagues. He also spent five seasons managing in the Yankees system. His big break came in 1944 when he switched from managing the Yankees' Binghamton farm team in the Eastern League to the Phillies' Utica farm team in the same league. He never was going to replace Joe McCarthy or Casey Stengel as manager of the Yankees. The Phillies, on the other hand, were another story.

In 1948 Sawyer had advanced from Utica to Toronto, the Phillies' top farm team in the International League, and he got the call to replace Ben Chapman in Philadelphia. It was a match made in baseball heaven. The Phillies were a young team and Sawyer, no doubt aided by his experience as a teacher, had earned a reputation for being especially effective with young players. In the minors he had managed Richie Ashburn, Granny Hamner, Jim Konstanty, Willie Jones, Stan Lopata, and Bubba Church; all of them were members of the big club when Sawyer arrived as manager.

In 1949 Sawyer led the young Phillies to their first winning season in 17 years. A year later, he guided the Whiz Kids to their first pennant in 35 years.

The 1950 pennant was such a high, it made the team's fall from grace that much more devastating. From 91 wins and first place in 1950, the Phillies plummeted to 73 wins and fifth place in 1951. By June 1952, the Phillies were in sixth place, seven games below .500, and Sawyer was replaced as manager by Steve O'Neill.

Sawyer stayed out of baseball but remained a hero in Philadelphia for his success in 1950. On July 22, 1958, with the team in seventh place under Mayo Smith, the Phillies reached out once again to Sawyer, hoping he could provide the same shot in the arm that he had given the team a decade earlier. It was not to be; the Phillies finished in last place in 1958 and 1959.

187

In 1950 Eddie Sawyer led the Whiz Kids to the Phillies' first pennant in 35 years.

As he prepared for the 1960 season in spring training, Sawyer's practiced eye could tell that there was little hope for a turnaround. The Phillies opened the season in Cincinnati and were blown away by the Reds 9–4. Sawyer could read the handwriting on the wall, and he didn't like what it said. Proving how truly intelligent he was, he resigned as manager of the Phillies.

Asked what prompted him to quit after only one game, Sawyer replied, "I'm 49 years old, and I want to live to be 50."

Eddie Sawyer never managed again. He lived to be 87.

Statistical Summaries

All statistics are for manager's Phillies career only.

MANAGING

G = Games managed
W = Games won
L = Games lost
PCT = Winning percentage
P = Pennants
WS = World Series victories

Manager	Years	G	W	L	PCT	P	WS
Charlie Manuel *Managed NL's first All Star Game victory in 14 years in 2010*	2005–11	1,134	646	488	.570	2	1
Dallas Green *His '81 club led NL in runs, hits, total bases, batting average, slugging, and on-base percentage*	1979–81	299	169	130	.565	1	1

continued	Years	G	W	L	PCT	P	WS
Gene Mauch *First manger to lead Philliesto winning records for more than four straight seasons (1962–67)*	1960–68	1,331	645	684	.485	0	0
Danny Ozark *Only Phillie manager through 2011 to win 100 games twice (1976–77)*	1973–79	1,105	594	510	.538	0	0
Eddie Sawyer *Had a 309–307 when he managed Phillies for a complete season (1949–51, 1959)*	1948–52, 1958–60	817	390	423	.480	1	0

Index

197

BOB BOONE • ANDY SEMINICK • DARREN DAULTON •
RYAN HOWARD • PETE ROSE • DOLPH CAMILLI • JIM
LAJOIE • JUAN SAMUEL • TONY TAYLOR • COOKIE RC
• GRANNY HAMNER • DAVEY BANCROFT • DICK BARTEI
JONES • PINKY WHITNEY • ED DELAHANTY • DEL ENN
RICHIE ASHBURN • CY WILLIAMS • BILLY HAMILTON • G
THOMPSON • ELMER FLICK • BOBBY ABREU • GAVVY (
ALEXANDER • JIM BUNNING • ROY HALLADAY • CURT S
• CURT SIMMONS • COLE HAMELS • JIM KONSTANTY •
MESA • CHARLIE MANUEL • DALLAS GREEN • GENE MA
ANDY SEMINICK • DARREN DAULTON • MIKE LIEBERTH
PETE ROSE • DOLPH CAMILLI • JIM THOME • EDDIE WAIT
• TONY TAYLOR • COOKIE ROJAS • MANNY TRILLO • JIM
BANCROFT • DICK BARTELL • MIKE SCHMIDT • DICK AI
ED DELAHANTY • DEL ENNIS • GREG LUZINSKI • PAT
WILLIAMS • BILLY HAMILTON • GARRY MADDOX • TON
FLICK • BOBBY ABREU • GAVVY CRAVATH • JOHNNY
BUNNING • ROY HALLADAY • CURT SCHILLING • STEVE
COLE HAMELS • JIM KONSTANTY • STEVE BEDROSIAN